بسم الله الرحمن الرحيم

The Hundred Steps

Shaykh
'Abd al-Qadir as-Sufi
ad-Darqawi

DIWAN PRESS

ISBN-13: 978-1-914397-16-5 (paperback)

978-1-914397-17-2 (ePub and Kindle)

Copyright © 1979 Diwan Press

This reprint 2021 CE/1443 AH

A catalogue record of this book is available from the British Library.

Published by: Diwan Press. 311 Allerton Road, Bradford, BD15 7HA, UK

THIS BOOK IS FOR THE FUQARA

'The pleasure of life is only in the company of the fuqara – they are the sultans, the masters and the princes . . . .

May I be reunited with them in Allah, and my wrong actions forgiven and pardoned by Him.

Then blessings be upon the Chosen, Sayyiduna Muhammad, the best of those who fulfilled and who vowed.'

Abu Madyan al-Ghawth

THE HUNDRED STEPS

1   **TASAWWUF**
2   SHARI'AT
3   TARIQAT
4   HAQIQAT
5   ADAB
6   ISTIQAMA
7   SULUK
8   YAQIN

9   **FAQIR**
10   TAWBA
11   WARA'
12   ZUHD
13   TAWAKKUL
14   SABR
15   SHUKR
16   TAQWA
17   IKHLAS
18   SIDQ

THE TREASURY OF TRUTHS

THE HUNDRED STEPS

Sufism is the science of the journey to the King.

Its preferred etymology is that it derives from suf, wool. Shaykh Hasan al-Basri said, 'I saw forty of the people of Badr and they all wore wool.' This means that the sufi – tasawwafa – has put on the wool. This is distinct from those who confirm the way of Islam with the tongue and by book learning. It is taking the ancient way, the primordial path of direct experience of the Real.

Junayd said: 'The sufi is like the earth, filth is flung on it but roses grow from it.' He also said: 'The sufi is like the earth which supports the innocent and the guilty, like the sky which shades everything, like the rain which washes everything.'

The sufi is universal. He has reduced and then eliminated the marks of selfhood to allow a clear view of the cosmic reality. He has rolled up the cosmos in its turn and obliterated it. He has gone beyond. The sufi has said 'Allah' – until he has understood. All men and women play in the world like children. The sufi's task is to recognise the end in the beginning, accept the beginning in the end, arrive at the unified view. When the outward opposites are the same, and the instant is presence, and the heart is serene, empty and full, light on light, the one in the woollen cloak has been robed with the robe of honour and is complete.

The Imam also said: 'If I had known of any science greater than sufism I would have gone to it, even on my hands and knees'.

'There is no road to the realities except on the tongue of the shari'at,' said Shaykh al-Akbar. The shari'at of Islam is the confirmation that there is no divinity but Allah and that Muhammad is the Messenger of Allah. It is to pray five times daily the ritual prostrations. It is to fast the month of Ramadan. It is to pay the zakat tax of wealth. It is to take, if possible, the Hajj to the pure House of Allah and the plain of Arafat. It is based on these and confirms that the one following the shari'at has elected to live within the broad moral parameters set down in the Qur'anic commands and according to the guidance within the sunna, the life-pattern of Muhammad, blessings of Allah and peace be upon him. Having accepted the shari'at is the deep cognition that the human creature is limited, is in a body, and thus, like all bodies in the physical world, obeys given laws. There is no compulsion in the life-transaction, thus it cannot be called 'organised religion' – no – it is the self-chosen pattern of life one has adopted in order to deepen knowledge until one reaches one's own source, one's spring of life, to drink of the water of illumination.

Shari'at thus implies recognition of biological laws that function at every level of existence. Thus, we observe that the kafirun, those who reject, nevertheless follow their shari'at. Every person sets up a shari'at, improvised yet functional. Our shari'at is all mercy, while theirs is always revealed to be cruel, repressive and narrow. Ours is from the Best of Creation, beloved by millions of human beings. Theirs is a dark shadow from lone imaginings.

The Path lies between the two opposites, shari'at and haqiqat. It is identifiable by its outward, and confirmed by its inward. Just as shari'at can also be called Islam, so tariqat may be called Iman – acceptance. Iman is acceptance. Iman is acceptance of Allah, His Books, His Messengers, His Angels, the Last Day, the Balance, the Decree. It is the interiorisation of the cosmic landscape, from creational realities in event, to a personal cosmic landscape in vision. All these explain and interpret the meanings of the dual nature of existence and its unitary secret.

Tariqat is a coming out from the safe place of ordinary existence into the alien existence of search, It means abandoning the private project as a meaning to life, that is, the family. Allah, glory be to Him, has warned that that is a trap for you. It means abandoning the public project which is the society and its promise of future rewards for slavery to it. The future reward of the seeker is now in the Unseen and after death, not at the end of life. It means abandoning the autobiographical project of fame and fulfillment, for the self has become for the seeker, an enemy. The self is an enemy, that is, until it is transformed into its luminous reality which is pure spirit, ruh.

Shari'at is submitting. Tariqat is handing over.
Haqiqat is victory.

Haqiqat, the realities, are the inward illuminations of knowledge which flood the heart of the seeker. It is the realm of meanings, as shari'at is the realm of the senses. As one is the science of the outward, the other is the science of the inward. There is no way to its experience but by submission to the fact of being human, being mortal, an in-time creature. Once shari'at is submitted to, then the seeker on the Path realises that he has come from non-existence and is going to non-existence. The time is short. It must be seized. Cut through! In this world everything is spectacle, yet everywhere the people are blind. They cannot bear to see that the world's rewards do not bring satisfaction to its people. This is not meant to be the zone of visions – that is the next world, after death. This is the zone of action. To reach the status of the whole human being is not possible without a breaking of norms. Breaking of norms is the Path. Its fruits are witnessing and illumination. Yet these belong to after-death in the sensory. Thus to reach vision in the meaning-realm means to die the death of meaning before the sensory death. 'Die before you die,' says the famous Hadith. It is re-iterated in many others from the Sahih, such as the instruction – 'Make yourselves as the inhabitants of the graves.' This does not suggest giving up life but that to know the great knowledge there must be practice – and that is its instruction.

If you desire haqiqat – reconcile yourself – your life can never be the same again. Man is asleep. 'When he dies he wakes up!' Haqiqat is waking up. Ihsan.

Adab is spiritual courtesy, sincere good manners. Adab implies sincerity and that implies humility. For if a person is aware of his manners then he is motivated by selfishness and is lacking in spontaneous expression.

Adab in the world is almost impossible. 'Correct manners' are practiced in the world. Adab is practiced in the circle of the People. Once in the protected circle of the People one has entered an arena of trust. Now adab is incumbent upon you. You have cornered the self – in the zawiyya, in the circle, among the Men of Allah, before the Shaykh. This is the arena of adab.

The Path is nothing but adab.

There is an adab due to the stranger and the visitor. There is an adab due the fuqara'. There is an adab due the noble and the elite. There is an adab due the Shaykh. The completion of adab is the adab due to yourself.

The first is arrived at by generosity and gifts at arrival and at departure. The next is marked by preference. You must prefer what you have or get, for your brother over yourself. The next is by service, and waiting, and patience, and listening. The next is wanting what your Shaykh wants, as if it were your wanting. The last is, in the first stage, the avoidance of the blow such as slapping the thigh or clenching the fist, and the avoidance of harsh exclamations. Its middle stage is the avoidance of extreme grief or joy. Its end is to have forgotten it altogether in the delight of the presence of the Real.

Istiqama is being straight. Its definition is to put in practice the sunna of the Messenger – his, words, his acts and his states – according to your knowledge of them and your capacity to follow them. Remember that no one can attain to his station of gnosis and radiance, while it is incumbent on us to follow in the dust of his footsteps.

Istiqama is taking on the character of one who fulfills the obligations. When someone washes and prays, when they fast and give sadaqa, when they move among the people of knowledge, when they visit the House of Allah, and the resting place of the Messenger, and sit in the Rowdah, they take on the colour of the people of these acts. By these acts even the bones become luminous. By these states, experienced among that company, the heart itself is illuminated.

It may seem outwardly to be narrow while the people of this world are outwardly broad – yet see how they are inwardly narrow while the people of istiqama are inwardly wide. Istiqama results in one who is outwardly dark and inwardly light, while the people of illusory freedoms are outwardly light while inwardly dark. The fruit of Istiqama is serenity while the fruit of unlimited behaviour is terror. One is sanity, the other is madness.

Suluk is the science of all the inward elements of wayfaring. The salik is the one who is grounded in the necessary wisdom to prevent insanity when the time comes that the heart moves and love awakens in it and the centre of the creature is possessed by the winds of yearning and the storms of longing. When the world and everything in it becomes for the seeker a torment and a trial it is suluk that holds the wayfarer to wisdom so that plunging is avoided when restraint is necessary and courageous action is possible when withdrawal is tempting. Suluk is the means by which the benefits of jadhb (attraction) become possible without becoming majdhoub, mad-in-Allah, that is, attraction can take place – for it is essential – and yet helpless attraction is avoided. That is to say, one may have the experience without being condemned to the station.

Our way is to be salik/majdhoub. Outwardly sane and inwardly mad-in-Allah. Outwardly sober and inwardly drunk.

Suluk is outwardly to replace bad speech with good speech, bad actions with good actions, bad intentions with good intentions, until one lives in right speech, action, and intention. The sign of the salik is that one is safe from his hand and his tongue, and the proof is that the salik is safe from his own hand and tongue.

Suluk allows one to benefit from the state by the absorption of the doctrine, and to leave the station in expectation of the further gifts of the Merciful Lord. Its term is return to its confirmation for the seekers, and avoidance of claim except on the tongue of the Real.

Yaqin, certainty, has three stages:
1) 'Ilm al-yaqin – knowledge of certainty.
2) 'Ayn al-yaqin – source of certainty.
3) Haqq al-yaqin – truth of certainty.

These may be considered as the deepening of three primary elements: shari'at, tariqat, haqiqat. Now we have moved from the conceptual to a further degree, that of experience. Now we are prepared to look on Islam and Iman and Ihsan not as propositions but rather as stages of direct life experience. The first is the capacity to accept the message and the Messenger. This is the foundation of one's humanity in the capacity to recognise and trust the genuine messenger. Trust of the true other is nothing less than the mirror act of self-trust. This leads to an inward confirmation of how-it-is, and therefore of oneself, as genuine. This middle term is vital to further development. You must confirm your own inwardness – it is the time of trial and the zone of departures. For man is weak and the middle is difficult. For the one with courage there is arrival at direct inner confirmation of the cosmic celestial realities and thus of the immutable jewel-essence of the self as being Light and not a shade dwelling in a decaying object, the body. The end is the truth of certainty. What is that? Our'an says it is death itself. Die the meaning-death and you arrive at the certain while in this life.

The Raja of Mahmudabad defined them thus:
You are told – there is a fire in the forest.
You reach the fire in the forest and see it.
You are the fire in the forest.

The Wali of Bahlil said: 'The fuqara' are a bunch of thorns.' Shaykh Abu Madyan said: 'The pleasure of life is only in the company of the fuqara – they are the sultans, the masters and the princes.' The faqir is the one who has turned from the futile search for this world and set out on the quest for the Real, that is, the secret of his own existence. The first requirement of this search is that he keep company with people who also wish to acquire this science. To be one of its people means to be beset with their difficulties and to gain their delight. At first the faqir sees the faults of the fuqara. When he learns that they are to him a mirror – as in the famous hadith – he ceases to struggle against them and love begins to grow in his heart for the lovers of Allah. By this means he approaches the Shaykh.

The faqir is poor in Allah, and Allah is enough for him in his poverty.

The faqir has opted for the war against the self. Thus he must set out on the most difficult part of his journey. Even success in it is dangerous, for contentment with acquiring good qualities is in turn a fault. There is no escape from it. Now he must break norms inwardly as he has already done outwardly. Wrong actions are gone. They must be replaced with right actions. So with intentions. The faqir, however, must guard against thinking that the goal is moral. Do not lose sight of the goal – it is direct witnessing of the living Lord.

Tawba – turning away from wrong action – is the beginning of the transformative process of the self. The middle is turning from wrong qualities to the right ones. The end is turning from creation to absorption in the vision of the Real.

The act of tawba is confirmed in the sunna of repeating one hundred times the supplication:

Astaghfirullah!

Sufyan ath-Thawri said: 'Real tawba has four signs: qilla: 'illa: dhilla: ghurba.' That is: decrease (of the self), weakness, humility, and exile (from the wrong).

Tawba is the sign to the faqir from himself that he has engaged in the battle. As long as the faqir persists in finding fault in others while failing to find fault with himself the journey has not even begun. The first engagement with wrong actions in tawba is a great victory. In one step the most difficult moment of the journey is over.

The common make tawba for wrongs: the elite make tawba for right actions and their praise: the elect of the elite make tawba for forgetfulness of Allah at any instant.

The proofs of the Path are the confirmations of the rewards of tawba, which confirm the seeker on his path and the people of arrival in the mercy of the Compassionate Lord.

Wara' – scrupulousness, in its lowest phase is avoidance of the haram and the doubtful. In its middle phase it is moving from the doubtful to what is certain to bring benefit. It is avoidance of anything that will cast a shadow on the heart. In its highest phase it is avoiding any desire except desire for Allah.

Hasan al-Basri was asked, 'What is the pivot of the deen (life-transaction)?' He replied: 'Wara'.'

If you are scrupulous with yourself and generous in judgement of others it is better for you than that you should be scrupulous in judgement of others and lax in your own behaviour.

The faqir must guard against contemplating his own scrupulousness, or basking in it, or resting in it, lest it too become a snare for him. Remember that there are people who make all the right actions and are careful in everything yet their hearts become hardened. The act of wara' is to release the self in its urgent quest for illumination and knowledge. It is a price to be paid, a tax to be levied, but joyously, and aware that it has nothing but benefits in it, for yourself and for others. So it has nothing in it to justify self-satisfaction, for it is for your own gain. If you rest in wara' – others are safe but you are not. If you make it a means – you are safe and others are taught.

Zuhd means doing-without. The Hadith (Ibn Majah, al-Hakim, Bayhaqi) says: 'Do-without the world – Allah will love you. Do-without what you find in the hands of men – men will love you.'

The zuhd of the sufis is that their doing-without should be an emptying of their hearts from desires of this world. Its aid is the emptying of their hands in sadaqa and generous gifts. The word 'ascetic' has nothing to do with zuhd as understood by Islam. Zuhd is a giving-up only when you have recognised that your need was a fantasy need. It is not zuhd to go in rags and to fast too much. Rather it would be zuhd to take care of clothes and patch them, or to eat less and not to eat one's fill. Zuhd is not, therefore, in any way a repression of appetites. It is an abandoning of excess appetite when the self has developed to the point of no long needing that thing.

To be zahid of objects is easy. To be zahid of words is more difficult, or the attention of others, or reputation. Do-without praise. Do-without reputation. Do-without being in the right. Do-without being seen. It is often easier for a king to be zahid than a poor man – beware!

The true zahid does-without a glance which sees creation and not the Lord.

Zuhd is easy. Its opposite is difficult. Remember the journey is to the place where the opposites have become the same for one. Do not dwell in the means – traveller – would you live in the stables?

Tawakkul. Reliance. The dhikr of this quality is strongly recommended for the faqir who is eager to move swiftly on the Path.

Hasbunallahu wa ni'amal wakil. Allah is enough for us and He is the Best Guardian.

Ibn Ajiba has said that the three degrees of tawakkul are. 1) Like the contracted one is with the contractor, so one is with the contractor, so one is with Allah – vigilant and concerned over his interests. 2) Like the child is with the mother – he turns only to her, in all things. 3) Like the dead body in the hands of the washer. The first has need in it, the second attachment, but the third is free of either need or attachment. This last is the station of those whose self has been wiped out, they wait only to see what He will do with them. These are the free.

Tawakkul gives strength to the faqir just as zuhd weakens the self in its energy for wrong actions. Tawakkul is nourishment, encouragement and sheer compassion from Allah to His slave in the difficult part of his journey. It is the dhikr of the moment when the faqir cannot go on. It is the dhikr for the moment of crisis when the faqir wishes to give up. It is the dhikr of trust for the moment when the faqir falters, sure he has made a mistake in ever imagining he can attain to the Real. If you set out you will arrive. Allah is enough for you. At the beginning. In the middle. At the end.

Repeat it inwardly for strength. Say it aloud to move forward. Shout it out, banging both fists on the table, to destroy all doubts and whisperings, and to subdue the most unruly self. Do it 73 times.

Sabr. Patience. Patience is a medicine which is bitter, whose fruits are sweet.

Our Imam has said that sabr is to be patient with patience.

The first patience to be learned is patience with others. This is the most difficult and if it is gained it is a great gain and a great victory. It has in it the seeds of forgiveness for others, and thus the noble quality of compassion before the weakness of human beings.

The second patience is patience with oneself. If one is harsh with the self it will wither. The self does not like to be treated harshly, let alone changed. The simple faqir will alter wrong actions first time round. The 'intelligent' who can argue and intellectualise can repeat wrong action several times before relinquishing it. The faqir must persist, again and again against the self. If he is patient – he will see the way to outwitting himself. The one who can do this has found a quick road and a sure victory.

The third patience is patience with the Decree of Allah – and it is to this that Imam Junayd refers. This is grappling with the very core of the doctrine of tawhid. This does not just refer to adversity and pain, such may even prove possible, or easy. What is difficult and vital is patience in the realm of event. 'Allah wants something. You want something. What you want is not what Allah wants, but know, that what Allah wants will certainly happen.' Patience in its fullness is wanting what Allah wants at every moment.

Shukr, giving thanks, is a knowledge and an encouragement. It makes you aware of the source of your life and it reminds you that He is the Answerer of prayers.

Its first degree is thanks with the tongue, which is dhikr. Its second degree is thanks with the whole body, which is service to Allah both in the prescription and in assisting His creatures. The third degree is thanks with the heart, which is thanks in the Presence of Lordship, and recognition in the audience chamber.

Shukr is the act due the slave. According to us shukr should never be expressed unless it is preceded with hamd. For hamd, praise, belongs entirely to Allah, it is His and the slave has no portion in it. Thus it is more fitting to present to Allah what has none of the slave in it before presenting what is entirely from the slave. If there has been du'a, then the shukr follows His answering it. If there has been no supplication then He has given the slave even without asking.

The dhikr of shukr therefore begins with hamd in every case, It should be repeated 100 times.

Al-hamdulillahi wa-sh-shukrulillah.

'No power, no strength but from Allah, the Exalted, The Vast.'

Shaykh Ibn Ajiba has said that the first degree of taqwa, guarding oneself, is the avoidance of wrong actions. Its second degree is the removal of faults, and its third degree is to turn from all that is other-than-Allah in order to withdraw into the Presence of the Knower of the Unseen.

One could say that the beginning of taqwa was the embracing of the moral parameters of the shari'at, while its middle was the deep acceptance of the self which Allah had allotted one so that its improvement and perfecting became the limit of one's interference in the world. The end of taqwa can then be seen as the arrival at the core, or at the centre of the circle of the self. Thus the end of taqwa is nothing less than khalwa, retreat, deep inner contemplation and the delight of witnessing the Lights of the attributes and the essence.

Far from making the human being a recluse or one who plays no part in the world the opposite is true. His arrow hits the mark. The man of taqwa is heard when he speaks, is copied when he acts, and illuminates others when he emerges. The man of taqwa has no fear of the creation, thus the world belongs to him and the elements are his willing servants. All his fear is placed in Allah, the Vast, the over-seer of his affair and the Mover in all his dynamic activities. Its dhikr is especially commended for travel. It is a dhikr most fitting in all matters concerning action and large movements involving many, like war.

La hawla wala quwwata illa billahi'l 'aliyyu'l-adhim

Ikhlas, pure unadulterated genuineness. The mukhlis is the one in whose sight there is always meeting with his Lord.

The definition is Surat al-Ikhlas itself. 'Say, Allah, He is the One. Allah He is Endlessly Rich (i.e. independent). He did not beget anyone and no-one begot Him. And He is not like anything.' Here is a definition of Allah on the tongue of the Real and it does not have in it anything of the slave. In it there is only Allah.

Once the faqir has reached the point that he can conceive of the human creature as containing these vast inner dimensions – once he realises that he is no longer a child of his time but rather a man of Time itself, once he grasps that given his possession of an intellect there is available to him a state unbounded then he knows his true self-form should be mukhlis.

The quick path to this condition is none other than the constant repetition of the Surat al-Ikhlas, and deep reflection on its tremendous meaning. Say it: 3 times. 111 times. 1000 times.

Bismillahir-Rahmanir-Rahim. Qul huwa'llahu Ahad. Allahus~Samad. Lam yalid wa lam yulad. Wa lam yakun lahu kufu'an Ahad.

The saddiqun are in the highest rank of the people of tawhid. Below them are the muqarrabun. The saddiq is true. Sidq is truthfulness. The one who is true has banished all hypocrisy and compromise. He is luminous, clear and cannot be corrupted.

The people of sidq have a perfume that is not of cleanliness or scents, but directly from the Garden of the Presence. Recognise such a man when you meet him. Sit in his presence. Take from him what he gives you in the way of guidance and admonishment. Lower your eyes. Do argue. Do not demonstrate your learning. What you have is nothing to what he has been given. It is a gift. The Messenger said, blessings and peace of Allah be upon him, speaking of Abu Bakr, that he was the first among his Companions not by any deed that he had performed, 'but because of something Allah had put into his heart.'

Its outward signs are ready trust, in Allah, in the Messenger, in the Books, the Angels, the Last Day, the Balance, and the Decree. This gives a ready trust in other men. This in turn engenders strong companions and sets up a noble community. The company of the saddiq is the perfect setting for contemplation and for witnessing. The dhikr for strengthening your portion of the greatest of qualities is the dhikr of acceptance of Allah and His vast power. It should be constantly on the tongue of the one who longs for this station.

Tabaraka'llah.

Our Master, the Shaykh al-Kamil, Sayyidi Muhammad Ibn al-Habib said:

"Murid is derived from 'irada (will) and it depends on Ikhlas. The true meaning of murid is one who has stripped himself of his own will and accepted what Allah wills for him, which is the worship of Allah, the Exalted, for He has said, 'I have not created jinn and men but to worship Me.' When the murid is weak in disciplining his self – since inner rule belongs to the self and Shaytan – he places himself under the rule of the Shaykh and in the protection of his power. He, in his turn, will help the murid to obey and worship Allah through his himma which operates by the permission of Allah, and through his words, which are made effective through the gift of Allah. So a murid must cling to whoever of the Shaykhs of the age are well disposed towards him.

Sidi Abd al-Wahad Ibn Ashir says: 'The murid keeps company with a Shaykh who knows the ways of behaviour and who protects him from danger on the way. The murid is reminded of Allah when he sees the Shaykh who then leads the slave to his Master.'

Ibn Ata-Illah, may Allah be pleased with him, says in his Hikam: 'Do not accompany one whose state does not change you and whose speech does not guide you to Allah.'

The elevation of your state and the guidance of his speech are the results of this companionship. So whoever does not find such a state from his companion let him abandon him to Allah and seek one of this description. The murid will gain a Master in accordance with his own sincerity and strength of resolution. Allah is the one to ask for help."

'Ubudiyya: slavehood. It has three degrees according to the Darqawa.

1) 'Ibadah. This is the realm of simple obedience which recognises all the obligations of the slave towards his Lord in all matters of worship.

2) 'Ubudiyya. This is slavehood. Here obedience is illuminated with pleasure in the service of the Lord. In the act of obedience is adab, deep spiritual courtesy. There is delight and confirmation of the necessary acts. There is a going beyond what is obligatory, and a willing expansion of the extra acts of worship such as night prayers, extra fasting, sadaqa, and the like.

3) 'Ubuda. This is sheer devotion. Shaykh Ibn Ajiba has defined it as being identical with spontaneous freedom itself.

Now in arriving at these three terms we have come to recognise a deepening of our original triad which in turn became a more profound concept of Yaqin. Here what was conviction yet still interior is actualised into the existential nature of the seeker. The faqir has taken on the responsibilities of being murid and has grasped that the whole matter of the Path is dependent on his own desire to arrive. Without acts nothing will happen. The acts of the seeker are defined above. The first is achieved when one has made the obligatory an ordinary part of life. The second when wudhu (washing for prayer) has become sweet for one. The third when the most loved thing in this world is the coolness of the eyes in prayer (salat).

Dhikr, invocation of Allah, is the great practice of the People. It has three degrees. To the common people it is dhikr of the tongue. To the elite it is dhikr of the heart. To the elect of the elite it is dhikr of the sirr, the secret. The first is well known. The second is dhikr accompanied by awareness so that the heart has become the arena of contemplation in the Presence of Lordship. The last is a tremendous affair. In it the tongue becomes mute and the heart still.

The first is dhikr of Huwa, the pronoun of absence. The second is the dhikr of Anta, the pronoun of presence. The third is the dhikr of Ana, the pronoun of tawhid.

Movement from the first stage to the second is marked by the body's agitation, such as swaying rhythmically, sudden exclamation, rising to the feet and so on. Movement from the second stage to the last is marked by the numbness of the limbs, and the silence of the tongue so that the dhikr becomes 'lost'. My Master, the Winepourer, Shaykh al-Fayturi said of this: 'What a wonderful thing! There were you looking for the dhikr! And there was the dhikr looking for you!'

In the Hikam it says: 'Do not abandon the dhikr because you fail to sense the Presence of Allah in it. Your forgetfulness of the dhikr of Him is worse than your forgetfulness in the dhikr of Him. Perhaps He will take you from a dhikr of forgetfulness to one with attention, and from one with attention to one with Presence, and from one with Presence to one in which everything but the Invoked is absent. And that is not difficult for Allah.'

Essential for the journey to Allah are three things. Dhikr is the first.

Fikr. Reflection.

Shaykh Ibn Ata-illah has said in his Hikam:

'Fikr is the voyage of the heart in the realm of otherness. Fikr is the lamp of the heart: when it goes away the heart has no illumination. Fikr is of two kinds: the fikr of confirmation and Iman, and the fikr of witnessing and vision. The first is for the people of examination and the second is for the people of vision and inner sight.'

'There are signs on the horizon and in the self': thus the first reflection should be the identification of Allah's Unity in the creation and the Command to be recognised in the cosmos. The second reflection should he a deep regard of the human self, the unity of its members, the hierarchy of its faculties, the immutability of the core awareness, and the inaccessibility of the 'I'. The third reflection takes place in the khalwa, in the deepest phase of muraqaba', watching. Here takes place the dislocation of the locus of observer, before the truth of our inability to see Him as it dissolves in the power of His witnessing us.

Dhikr is sensory: fikr is meaning. Dhikr is outward: fikr is inward.

Essential for the journey to Allah are three things. Fikr is the second.

Essential for the journey to Allah are three things. Himma is the third. Shaykh Ibn al-Habib says in his famous Diwan: 'Whoever has got dhikr, fikr, and himma will in each moment rise above otherness. He will attain gnosis beyond his desire and fast realise the secrets of existence.'

He also says: 'Awaken your himma with yearning and longing, and do not be content with less than the Ever-continuing!' He further says: 'And, oh my companion, himma is the possession to have, then if you desire the goal of all the gnostics you can set out for it.'

Himma – aspiration, is defined by Shaykh al-Akbar as follows: 'It is applied to correspond to freeing the heart by desire. It is applied to correspond to the beginning of the sincerity of the murid. It is applied to correspond to all himma by the purification of yearning.'

Shaykh Ibn al-Habib referred to it as the mount of himma, for it is by himma that you travel the Path. It is itself that impulse of the heart which moves the seeker first to seek a guide and then to acquire the basis of the art. Then, once he has become accomplished in the practice a torpor settles over the heart of the seeker, for he has mistaken the means for the end. It is himma which rouses the seeker again, for the difficult middle passage of the Way. In the middle of the Path it must be remembered that what is himma then will change radically, for in the end it will be nothing less than desire to return to the audience chamber for the wine of witnessing and the greeting of the Beloved.

In the beginning it is aspiration to acquire the sciences. In the middle it is aspiration to arrive at direct experiences. In the end it is aspiration to be granted further gnoses in witnessing and absorption in the vision of the Lord.

This triad defines the human creature in their gnostic totality. The first level of experience of the human animal is that of nafs. Awareness of selfhood is the basic necessary condition for the journey. Without it, that is, if majnun (mad), you cannot embark. Unless there is a functioning locus of experience it is not possible to arrive at its dislocation in the act of self-discovery.

Shaykh al-Akbar defines nafs as: 'What is caused of the attributes of the slave.' So it is that the self is imprisoned by the very elements it imagines liberate it – actions. The more the self does the more it builds up an illusory continuity and history. Event consolidates the myth of the self. This is why Shaykh al-Kamil says that everything in the nafs is dreadful. It is irrelevant to imagine you can 'forge' a good nafs. It is a more terrible idol than the bad one. The nafs is the great idol which, while it sets up the other idols cannot smash itself. This is why one takes a Shaykh. His function is simply to serve as a mirror self which will help one escape the deceptions of the self which are self-perpetuating.

The goal of the People is the annihilation of the experiencing self.

The practice of the People is dhikr by which the heart is purified so that what was the solid and opaque nafs becomes subtle and luminous. Once the dhikr and the keeping company have subdued the nafs the seeker is able to discern that the locus of the human creature is not what it had seemed. In place of the narrative fiction of the self he is able to discern a direct biological identity. At this stage he refers not to nafs but to ruh.

Ruh means spirit. Shaykh al-Akbar defines it as: 'Ruh – it is applied to what casts knowledge of the Unseen to the heart in a particular aspect.' We notice that the organ of experience in both cases, and the one that follows, is the heart. But now, the locus is recognised in its natural form not in its historic form. It is not any more thought of as an event-locus but rather as a vision screen. Thus what was the arena of action becomes the arena of sight.

Shaykh Ibn al-Habib says in his Diwan: "My rub speaks to me and says: 'My reality is the light of Allah, so do not see other-than-Him. If I were not a light I would be other-than-Him, indeed otherness is nothingness, so do not be content with it.'"

Once this recognition has dawned, it remains for the seeker to realise the secret of the ruh. He must discover his original self, his adamic face.

This is the last stage of gnosis and at this stage the ruh must be designated by another name, appropriate to these meanings. So we see that here the triad which defines the most intimate and personal realm of self experience is none other than what earlier defined only concepts and belief patterns.

Sirr, the secret.

This is the third delineation of self locus. Look at the fine definition of the Shaykh al-Akbar and understand it. He said:

'It is applied, and they say that the sirr of knowledge corresponds to the gnosis of the one who knows it, and the sirr of the state corresponds to the gnosis of what Allah desires in him, and the sirr of the reality to what indication brings.

It must now be clear to the seeker that what had begun as an 'autobiographical' search to find the meaning of his 'historical' existence has now been swept away. He is no longer able to see himself as a narrative figure. He is immersed in a natural study of himself in which he looks at his condition as the biologist examines the organism in its environment. What he discovers himself to be is a knower, a knower whose capacity can be deepened and deepened so that at each stage of the way he must jettison all he knew before. Then his 'life' could be said to come to an end as his knowledge begins. The sufi lives posthumously. Unattached, he is able to taste the finer and finer meanings of the self/cosmos locus. The first zone of the sirr is active, and involves capacity to grasp what is shown and to hold to himma for Allah alone. The second zone is passive. Here all guides are left behind. This knowledge is arrived at in the depths of muraqaba, watching. The third zone is so subtle it cannot be talked about except in coded language such as that used by the Sultan of the Lovers, Shaykh Ibn al-Farid. It is active/passive. It holds the unitary discovery. It is called sirr-as-sirr. The secret of the secret. Shaykh al-Akbar defines it: 'That by which Allah is isolated from the slave.'

Mulk – the kingdom of solid forms.

Now alongside the triad which outlines the self-locus we place a triad which outlines the three worlds of existence, or if you prefer, the three modes of existence in the Universe.

The first realm is the mulk. The visible realm. The mulk is what is experienced in the sensory (hiss) and in illusion (wahm). Of its nature mulk is both solid, sensory, and pure-space, illusory. This is now confirmed by kafir science. The amazing interlocking substantiality of mulk veils most people from the meaning-realm onto which it opens the intellect, thus it is designated kingdom for it is a realm of reality, seemingly complete in itself. It is not real, but it is made with the Real, in the language of Qur'an. Thus to understand it we must penetrate its imprisoning solidity. Since we are in it and of it, it must be expected that breaking the mulk barrier will also blow apart the experiencing locus of the self. We are now able to say that facing the mulk is the nafs. With nafs the creature remains in it and by it. We do not dismiss the mulk for it is the direct evidence of the King. Our search will return us to it. What we want is an encompassing knowledge for we do not seek to 'understand the universe' like the pathetic kafir who tries to list everything in existence! In the words of Rabe'a al-'Adawiyya, 'Do not seek the garden, seek the gardener.'

By using the faculty of cognition we realise that everything in the mulk is coded meanings – this opens the self to the next realm.

The limits of the mulk are the limits of concepts and thought-forms.

Malakut – the kingdom of Unseen forms.

This is both the kingdom of the source-forms of the creational realities, crystals, atoms, organisms, and the kingdom of the spiritual realities, the Lote-tree, the Balance, the Throne and so on. It is the realm of vision as the mulk is the realm of event. As the characteristic of the mulk is fixity or apparent fixity so the characteristic of the malakut is flux and transformation or apparent flux. In fact one could say that the reality of the two worlds is opposite that, for indeed the solid forms are all in change, while the visions are all unfolding the fixed primal patterns on which all the visible world is based.

Once the malakut opens its treasures to the seeker he must beware becoming a child of its wonders as the kafir remains a child of the wonders of the mulk. One can never be content with anything except the arrival at the audience chamber of the Real. The malakut is what is experienced in knowledge and dhawq, tasting. Everything in malakut is decoded/sensory. Thus the vision of the Garden is houris, youths, rivers and gardens. The sensory in the mulk is experienced intellectually through low level cognitions. In the next world after-death is experienced through high level perceptions.

The limits of the malakut are the limits of vision.

Jabarut – the kingdom of power. This is the kingdom of lights. Shaykh al-Akbar notes: 'With Abu Talib it is the world of Immensity. With us it is the middle world.' By this he indicates that the mulk is opposite the malakut and it is precisely the realm of lights Divine Presence that creates the split between the two worlds on which creational reality is based. That means that Light is the barzakh, the inter-space between the visible and the invisible. In reality existence is one, the three kingdoms are one kingdom with one Lord. It is by the setting up of the limits and the barriers and the differences that the universal metagalactic existence is able to come into being. That which sets up the barriers, and is the barriers, is none other than the One Reality in its sublime perfection unrelated to any form. The barriers are not realities in themselves yet without them nothing would be defined and no-one could define them.

Qur'an declares that Allah, glory be to Him, is the Outwardly Manifest and the Inwardly Hidden: the First and the Last. Wherever you turn there is the face of Allah. Allah is the light of the heavens and the earth. By light we discriminate and by light we are blinded into non-discrimination. Both separation and gatheredness depend on light.

Jabarut is light upon light.

In his prayer on the Messenger, Shaykh al-Mashish says: 'Oh Allah bless the one out of whom the secrets have burst and the lights have flooded. By him realities arose and the knowledge of our Master Adam, peace be upon him, descended on him. So the creatures are incapable beside him, and understanding is a trifle to him. Not one of us has attained to his level before or after. The gardens of the malakut are delighted by the flowers of his beauty, and the basins of the jabarut are overflowing with the effusion of his lights.'

Khawf means fear, dread of the Creator and the Master of the Day of Judgement. During the faqir's times he reflects on the way in which creational realities work. He examines the human situation, not as legend or history but rather with the Qur'anic perspective of peoples who built great societies and were all swept away by the vast inexorable surge of time over the cosmic space, itself more vast than can be held in the intellect. He realises that the disaster on the street can scarcely be recognised from a high building let alone a plane. He realises that the passions of his parents' youth are already unreal and inaccessible even to them. He takes cognisance of the smallness of the caravan and the vastness of the desert. From this reflection dread awakens in the heart for the tremendous power of the Creator. Yet as khawf develops, fear of creation disappears. It is not possible to fear Allah without recognising His promise to His slaves. This connects to the next quality, for the two are inseparable and should be balanced. Excess of khawf would result in one who dared not speak or move. This would be an abandonment of knowledge. The one we fear is the compassionate Lord. Fear in the beginning is a knowledge. Fear in the middle is an ignorance. Fear at the end is a delight. As the fire is compatible to the nature of the salamander, so is the power of the inexorable Lord to the helpless and contented slave.

Opposite khawf is raja' – these two move the seeker by a dynamic, so that by them he advances on the Path.

Raja' is hope.

The salih who brought Shaykh Ibn al-Habib to the sufic Way used to climb the steep steps of their Fez lodging house declaring, 'Khawf! Raja'! Khawf! Raja'!' with each step. By this he indicated the perfect and balanced approach to knowledge to the young scholar who still lived in the frozen realm of concepts and dialogue.

Hope at the beginning is the longed for good that will come after death in the rewards of the Garden. In the middle it is Allah's satisfaction with His slave. In the end it is clear vision of the King and entry into knowledge of His secrets.

Shaykh Ibn al-Habib says in his Diwan: 'You must put on the twin sandals of fear and hope.'

The encounter with these opposites is a necessary stage of the way. It cannot be avoided. Do not seek to lessen the inexorable and terrible majesty of Allah because He may have sheltered you from some of His majestic acts. Do not slip into a childlike understanding of what compassion is. The knife of the surgeon is also compassionate. Anguish in this world is a compassion if by its lessons we avoid anguish in the next.

It must be that the faqir becomes established in khawf and raja'. A time will come when these two knowledges will transform into yet a deeper and more illuminating experience.

Rida' – serene content.

It is the pivotal condition of the one who has balanced his fear and his hope. The one who has gained rida' is the one who has broken through the clash of the opposites in the sensory world. The common people laugh when happy and cry when sad. They call on Allah in difficulty and forget Him when all goes well. Or they acknowledge Him when it is easy and at the first sign of trial rush here and there trying to deal with things.

Beware in case you think of the man of rida' as being passive and inactive. This is the claim of the kafir and the ignorant one. Rida' frees man to act where his actions will take effect. Rida' will guide a man to speech when his speech will be heard and acted upon. Equally it will guide him to silence or stillness when there would be no point in taking issue. The one who is content with Allah is not concerned over the opinions of others, either their approval or their disapproval See what a tremendous step this is in the liberation of the self.

Shaykh Ibn Ajiba designates three stages of rida':

1) The common people – for them it is patience and inner struggle.

2) The elite – for them it is the end of bitter and turbulent thoughts.

3) The elect of the elite – for them it is joy, absence of agitation, and serenity.

Hiss, sensory, is existence as solidifications, thicknesses, while ma'na, meaning, is existence as subtleties, therefore things in themselves have no thing-ness, for they are not, until they are recognised. Once they are recognised they are transformed by the one who cognises them. Thus hiss is in continual transformation into ma'na. One cannot be considered without the other. Shaykh Moulay Abd al-Qadir al-Jilani has compared the universe to snow, whose separate individual myriad forms are in reality one water. Each condition is true and each according to the laws governing what may be indicated from that point of view.

Sidi Ali al-Jamal says in the *The Meaning of Man*: 'Know that sensory things are two: things and their opposites. Similarly, things of meanings are two: things and their opposites. Each of them is the existence of the thing... The Lord of sensory things is the Lord of meanings. The judgement on sensory things is the judgement on meanings. The cure of meanings is the cure of sensory things, although meanings are gathered-ness and sensory things are separated. The gatheredness of gatheredness gathers all. The gatheredness which gathers what is gathered is true, and what separates what is separated is true by a truth in a truth of a truth.'

At this stage it is incumbent on the faqir to recognise that things and therefore event (interaction of things) are not explicable in terms of themselves but must be decoded into their meanings. As with the great triad of shari'at, tariqat, haqiqat, the faqir will move from this dual opposite to a deeper terminology as he progresses from doctrine to experience.

Ma'na is meaning. Sidi Ali al-Jamal has said: 'All creation, good and corrupt, witnesses Allah. However, they do not recognise Him, and they do not see the Real as the Real and recognise Him except for the one whose heart has the light of meanings. These lights of meanings by which Allah is seen and recognised only appear in the heart by the exaltation of the senses intending to seek Allah. Similarly, the darkness of meanings only appears by the illumination of the senses because wisdom is not in witnessing. It is in gnosis, because Allah is manifest to everyone, hidden to everyone. The gnostic is the one who recognises Him in the outward as he recognises Him in the inward and recognises Him in the inward as he recognises Him in the outward. As for the one who recognises Him outwardly and not inwardly, or recognises Him inwardly and not outwardly, he is ignorant. The ignorant is not called gnostic. Shaykh ash-Shushtari, may Allah have mercy on him, said:

> Do not look at vessels.
> Dive into the sea of meanings.
> Perhaps you will see Me
> In the company of the sufis.

The meanings become a condition of seeing, and exalting the senses becomes a condition in the manifestation of meanings. Directing consciousness to seeking Allah becomes a condition in darkening the senses. Allah gives success!'

It must now be clear that the faqir is already embarking on a knowledge process by which he may understand the very texture of cosmic/self existence. At this stage he must equip himself with a new set of doctrines which will clarify for him the zones of intellection and their gnosis as they open up to him through his intensified practice of 'directing consciousness to seeking Allah.'

Lubb, core – is a Qur'anic term. Shaykh al-Akbar defines it as: 'The matter of divine light.'

In the first stage of our Path we look on the whole outer form of the self as it is then experienced, a bundle of dirty rags and garbage. The self is fought with the weapons of purification – salat, fasting, right action, most of all, sadaqa. It is cleansed of its impurities by travelling in the way of Allah and keeping company with the purified. Now the faqir has zeroed in on what is at the heart of this bundle of contradictory and worthless energies. By his dhikr and fikr, his himma has taken him to the realm of concentration. Whereas in the beginning he sat in the sama'a as at a spectacle, observing its courtesies and enjoying its beauty, now his eyes are lowered, his thoughts are stilled and his concentration is on his own beating heart ('for there are not two hearts in the breast') as he waits for lights to enter into it. It is at this stage that he moves from a static view of the heart as a lump, however active and receptive, to a different view of its characteristics. As the gnostic instrument he now must look on it as his lubb, his core. What is the core? It is not only the centrality of the thing but it in turn 'contains' the whole pattern of the complete organism, just as the core of the apple contains the seed which is tree, blossom, fruit and seed itself. Hadith Qudsi: 'The whole universe cannot contain Me but the heart of the mu'min contains Me.'

Ishara – indication.

It is defined by Shaykh al-Akbar thus: 'It may be with nearness, and with the presence of the Unseen, and it may be with distance.'

By this the teacher implies that for full experience of Ishara there must be enlightenment about the knowledge it points to, otherwise it is merely metaphor and concept. Ishara therefore is a gnostic event if it is effective. Shaykh Ibn Ata-illah says in his Hikam: 'The gnostic is not the one who, when he makes an indication finds Allah nearer to himself than his indication. Rather the gnostic is the one who has no indication due to his annihilation in His existence and self-absorption in contemplating Him.' By this we realise that the indications are means for the refining of the understanding, the sharpening of the eye, the purification of the contemplation, the dissolving of the barriers, the refining of the meanings. They are the ferry across the river of fikr from the bank of the sensory to the bank of the meanings.

It is said: 'Our science is all indications. When it is stated, it disappears.'

Ishara is the coded language of the lovers used to lure the seeker into the realm of delight and witnessing, used to revive the ruh to return to the homeland of love. It is the language of the great Diwans: it speaks of Layla, of moons, of cups and wine. It is this science that only now can be approached by the awakening seeker as the goal comes nearer at last.

Waqt – the moment.

Shaykh al-Akbar has defined it thus: 'It designates your state at the time of the state. It is not connected to the past or the future.' By this deep and specific definition it can be seen that the moment is not the 'instant-of-time'. It is that moment when the Real is recognised. The waqt is the cutting edge of the sword yet neither the right nor the left side of the blade. (At this point the faqir should be warned against applying the sufic scientific vocabulary outside its zone of action in ordinary affairs as this will destroy his progress.) It is said: 'The sufi is the slave of the moment.' By that is meant that he is always aware and ready to recognise the Real in what the Real has brought him at that moment. There are therefore no impingements, rather there is only the Real, so when the moment is recognised it is as if the seeker had awakened from the sleep of ordinary perception. The term is used in the plural in the sense of 'times set aside': we say – build up the times. This means set aside more and more time for dhikr with fikr. Increase your himma to be watchful for the immediate Presence. From now on all that is happening is that the seeker is becoming aware of the vital reality of the lived moment. The future is the positive pole and the past the negative, brought together they are constantly transforming into the electrical charge of the present. This kind of awareness is based on dhikr and fikr and himma. Its most powerful technique at this stage is long hadra (or raqs: the dance of the breath).

Hal – state.

Shaykh al-Akbar defines it: 'It is what occurs to the heart without reliance or procuring. If it goes on, like may not follow it. Whoever makes like follow it, speaks of its constancy. Whoever does not make like follow it, speaks of its lack of constancy. It is said that the state alters attributes for the slave.'

At this stage of experience the faqir has now entered into the arena of contemplation and its fruits. Hal does not come from event, or from outside, or from feelings, or from nafs in any of its modalities. Hal descends on the heart, and as we have noted it is itself in motion, changing at every instant. The faqir must learn to move with its motions as the sailor changes sail with the winds. Do not tell what comes on the heart to others. From this point on the faqir must report his inner experiences only to his Shaykh, or to a recognised one among the salihun.

It has been said: 'It begins as a madness: its middle is science: its end is stillness.' That is: *junun, funun, sukun.*

Hal puts in motion what was still, then it calms it, and finally gives it rest. These are the effects of love. Now, only now, can we talk of love for the first time.

Maqam station.

Shaykh al-Akbar says of it: 'It designates fulfilling the rights of the rules completely.' That is to say, the maqam is arrived at when the slave is established in a degree of adab in his khidma, service to Allah, and when he has acquired a firm place in certainty inwardly. Stations first manifest, fleetingly, as ahwal (pl. of hal), then they become fixed in the murid. This is likened to dyeing cloth, so that it is dipped in the same colour and dried, dipped and dried, until the colour at a certain point becomes fixed. Once the dye is fixed the maqam is established.

The seeker moves from maqam to maqam. By then he rises in knowledges and gnoses, they are the 'degrees' mentioned in Qur'an. In turn, the maqamat of the great can be a snare and a temptation. If they are a temptation for the lovers think what a disaster word of them is for the scholar who has never had scent of them. We pray Allah to keep you among the people of 'amal, (actions). If the seeker is in the hands of a gnostic Shaykh then he will not leave his murid lingering in the stages but will hasten him on to the meeting place of recognition as the hajjis must hasten on to the waymarks of Allah in the pure valley. Once you hear a breath of the language of the stations, cling to your Shaykh, look no more with the eye, but watch with the heart. Drink from his source, take his cup when it comes to you. Yearn passionately now for the Beloved.

Mawqif – stopping-place.

This is a most useful and salutary term. It is a stopping-place. The mawqif is that stopping-place between stations. As Muzdalifa is the stopping-place between Arafat and Mina, so also is the mawqif the place between two maqamat. Just as in Muzdalifa you do not rest much, neither do you in the mawqif. The duties of Muzdalifa are twofold. One is the gathering of the pebbles for the stoning of the Shaytans on reaching Mina, and the other is making supplication as the sun rises before setting out for Mina. Thus, without the halt there, you would have no stones for the stoning of the Shaytan, nor would you be able to supplicate Allah for what the heart most desires. It is a rest and a gathering place, and a place of helplessness.

It is said that in the mawqif the faqir loses all that he has gained up until that moment, and has not yet acquired what will come to him in the next stage. Like a person in the baths who sheds his soiled clothes, is naked, and is dependent on the bath attendant to give him clean clothing, so the faqir is helpless in the generous power of his Lord.

Its requirements are humility, increased adab, recitation of Qur'an and much supplication.

In the mawqif the faqir is well aware of his condition. He realises how far Allah, glory be to Him, has taken him. His yearning increases. He takes stock. It increases him in praise and thanks. He knows at that moment the worth of all he has experienced, and he returns to his journey longing for the goal.

Warid – is what descends on the heart of Lights indicating the Absolute Lord of Majesty and Generous gifts. Ya dha'l jalali wa'l-'ikram!

Warid is overflowing, which floods the heart of the seeker, so that the limits of his experiencing self spill out and he knows that the self is not confined to the limits of his own skin but takes in all that is within his perception, objects, persons and place. He knows no separation between them and him, all this without feeling, for the self is flooded by light. What well up in the heart are the first indications of the love that he may still think flows from him to existence, but in truth, flows over existence engulfing him. All actions become his actions, all others have his spirit. This is the first dissolution of the barriers of separation. He is temporarily without time, space melts, and he tastes from the sea of Oneness.

When the seeker is visited by warid and has reported it to his Shaykh, he will find it made little of by his Master, this is to protect him from self-admiration and arrogance. The results of the warid lie further off and it is a time for consolidation. Allah overwhelms us so we must turn to the Salat an-Nabiy. Allahumma salli wa salem ala Sayyidina Muhammadin wa 'alihi bi 'adadi kulli ma'alumin lak. 'Allah bless our Master Muhammad and his family according to the number of all created things' 1000 times.

Hikam says: 'Do not attest to the validity of a warid whose fruits you do not know. The purpose of rain-clouds is not to give rain: their only purpose is to bring out the fruit.'

Futuwwa – nobility.

Futuwwa is to think outwardly not of yourself but only of the muslims. Inwardly it is to be concerned only for Allah. It is the intrinsic virtue of the Messenger, blessings of Allah and peace be upon him.

Abu'l Husayn al-Warraq of Nishapur said: 'Futuwwa has five qualities: fulfilling the contract, trustworthiness, thankfulness, patience and serene contentment.'

Futuwwa indicates the faqir becoming a universal man. His allegiance is no longer local, neither to family nor to friend nor to country. His family are the umma, that is the whole community, and the rest of mankind are his guests. With this perspective on the world he is free to give himself to Allah entirely.

The faqir has arrived at the middle of the Path.

Qabd – constriction.

Shaykh al-Akbar says of it: 'It is the state of fear. It is the moment (waqt). It is called a warid which comes on the heart. It demands the indication of rebuke and discipline. It is said: 'the warid of the moment reproached.' Qabd is the state of fear. Just as khawf was the experience of the beginner on the Path now the seeker has deepened his understanding of the life-process. Fear is caused by encounter with the world, and its enormity, as if alien to the self. Now that the faqir realises that the world is before him as a mirror and that what issues from it is from his own heart then his fear is not of how Allah will deal with him through His mighty power in creation but with qabd the seeker experiences contraction inwardly and it may or may not relate to the outer.

Qabd is meaning. It is the residue of burned up hopes that were vain. All qabd, as experience, is direct apprehension of death. Azra'il, the bringer of death, is of course, an angel. Angels are light. So we may say that qabd is a forgetfulness and a weakening of certainty. That is why the Shaykh al-Akbar warns that it calls for rebuke and discipline.

Qabd is sometimes claimed because of the inability of the seeker to experience lights, but there is a reason for this, and it is that he still is in opposites and has failed to see the One Lord in what the Lord has given him. Shaykh Ibn Ata-illah said in the Hikam: 'He expanded you so as not to keep you in contraction, and contracted you so as not to keep you in expansion and He took you out of both so that you do not belong to anything apart from Him.'

Bast – expansion.

Shaykh al-Akbar defines it: 'With us it is whoever is wide enough for things, and nothing is wide enough for him. It is said that it is the state of hope. It is said that it is a warid, and it demands the indication of mercy and intimacy.'

As qabd is the meaning of fear so bast is the meaning of hope. It is important to realise the move in consciousness that the faqir has made from sensory to meaning. For while the sensory is still connected to nafs and event, the meaning moves one to the ruh and vision.

Each hal demands an adab in it and an adab following it. Shaykh Ibn Ata-illah said in the Hikam: 'It is more dreadful for gnostics to be expanded than to be contracted, for only a few can stay within the limits of adab in expansion.'

Its dhikr in it is: Subhanallahi wa bi-hamdihi – Subhanallahi al-'adhim. 21 times.

The dhikr in qabd is always in every case hadra and recitation of Qur'an at length.

Wajd – is the first degree of ecstasy. These three terms all derive from the root of w-j-d. It means to find oneself, to find, to desire deeply, to exist. This permits us to say that the root of existence is itself ecstasy.

Shaykh al-Akbar defines it: 'It is what the heart unexpectedly encounters of its unseen states withdrawn from witnessing.'

The second degree of ecstasy is called wijdan. Shaykh Ibn Ajiba defines it as being when the sweetness of witnessing lasts, accompanied usually by drunkenness and bewilderment.

With both these conditions something of the inner state spills out and floods over the gathering. While some sufis permit the acting of ecstatic states with the intention that they may be arrived at, such behaviour was strictly forbidden in the company of the Shaykh al-Kamil who considered men today already vulnerable to neurotic states of distraction. If the hal is real it is the duty of the salihun among the People to soothe and guide the person back to calm, without force or harm. Repetition of the Names of mercy can alone work wonders on the distracted heart. We came upon a majdhouba at the wall of the Ka'ba in wijdan, the fierce jalali power of the House had invaded her and she was distraught. By the recitation to her of 'Ya Rahman – Ya Rahim' repeatedly she almost immediately left what had been a shattering state. Recitation of the Our'an will in every case restore the distracted one, but Allah knows best.

Wujud is the third degree of ecstasy. In wujud awareness dominates bewilderment and reflection irradiates force. The mark of wujud is that one experiencing it is aware enough to be concerned to hide it from his brothers and to avoid attracting attention not just for the sake of adab to others but out of adab to the state that it may be deepened and enjoyed. It is vital that the seeker should on no account be embarrassed or attempt to repress a state of wajd of whatever degree. Since we do not permit simulated wajd (called tawajud) by the same token we do not steal the states of others. When wajd descends, withdraw. It is not possible to 'experience' these states and in them the Watcher is as damaging as the Railer, who would decry it as worthless. These are two roles that the nafs takes to deny the seeker the lights of gnosis. Equally when wajd descends it is too late to do dhikr. It was for this the dhikr or sama'a took place. This is a Presence, and in the Presence there is no longer need to call upon, for the adab of Presence is prostration and the prostration of the wujud is the prostration of the heart.

Imam Junayd, our leader, said:

'Wujudi an aghiba ani'l-wujūd bimā yabdū 'alayya mina'l-shuhūd'

'My wujud is that I absent myself from existence because of what is shown to me in the witnessing.'

So Shaykh al-Akbar sums it up as: 'Wujud (finding) is experiencing the Real in wajd (ecstasy).'

Jadhb – attraction.

The majdhoub is the one of Divine attraction. This term is common in the Darqawi Way and is sometimes used too lightly. The faqir must fear the power of Allah and His attraction. One is drawn to it and yet repelled with the Messenger's horror of insanity, since it is precisely the intellect that is the necessary faculty for gnosis. This is why the Wali of Bahlil warned that the adab towards the majdhoub was 'As-salaamu alaikum – and then beat it!' The one who keeps company with the majdhoub will become majdhoub or the servant of the majdhoub, for their power is enormous, since their intellect is nowhere it is, of course, everywhere. Yet brief contact with the great majdhoubs is enormously rewarding and advances the seeker towards his goal. There are some majdhoubs who are salik/majdhoubs, obeying the shari'at and keeping the bounds while plunging into the depths of the Divine ocean, but these are rare.

Beware of majdhoub tales, while failing to long for a jadhb with knowledge. Our Junaydi Way is to be outwardly sober and inwardly drunk. Shaykh al-Fayturi said to us: 'What greater jadhb than to have crossed the world to enter khalwa under me. For your jadhb takes you to ma'rifa, witnessing and wilayat. That is the jadhb to acquire. Passionate yearning for the winepourer.'

Shaykh Ibn al-Habib said: 'Many are called majdhoub, but the real majdhoub is the one who prays dhuhr in the Great Mosque in Meknes, prays asr in Makkah at the Ka'ba and is back in Meknes for maghrib!'

Lawa'ih – outward gleams.

Shaykh al-Akbar has said of them: 'It is what shines from the outward secrets, from the height, from a state to a state. With us, it is what shines to the eye when it is not limited by the outside and from the lights of tasting, not from the direction of the heart.'

Here are indicated the first breaks in awareness. They are flashes, dazzling bursts that seem to break in on a dark scene. These must be discounted at all costs. In the first motions of what we term the dislocation of the watcher there are inevitable physiological effects. The outer eye must stop sending images if the inner eye is to function in the heart. Yet the tremendous rapidity of change from outer sensory terrestrial to inward sensory celestial trails with it like a slipstream, impulses from the body and the nervous system. This is not yet, however, inner meaning celestial, which is what we intend.

This is what is meant in the Diwan of Shaykh Ibn al-Habib when he says, using another term: 'Do not stop at the first gleams, nor with anything else you may experience at this stage.'

Shaykh Ibn Ata-Illah says in the Hikam: 'Sometimes lights come upon you and you find the heart filled with images of created things so they return from where they descended.'

Al-Lawami' – gleams.

Defined by Shaykh al-Akbar as: 'What is constant of the lights of tajalli for two moments or near that.'

Where the lawa'ih lights are designated as from the foundation of the state in the body, here the lawami' lights are recognised as, not sensory, but meaning, thus apprehended in the ruh on the screen of the sensory, by the ruh.

It is at this stage that the mature faqir realises that here in these illuminations are the first indications of what man is for, man is a locus of lights. 'We have not created jinn and men except to worship Us', declared by the Real, glory be to Him. Our Messenger has confirmed that a worship with knowledge is higher than a worship without it, and witnessing is a knowledge higher than information. These first genuine lights that come upon the longing heart of the slave are indications that the Path's realities are being won, and that reunion is near, and that witnessing is inevitable, and that Allah answers the prayers of His slave. Let your prayers be for Him and not His fruits either in the visible world or in the Unseen. Seek only the Face of Allah. Go on.

At-tawali' – splendours.

These are defined by Shaykh al-Akbar as: 'The lights of tawhid shining on the hearts of the people of gnosis so that they obliterate all other lights.'

The tawali' lights are the fruits of muraqaba, of watching. At this stage it is enough to know that from the lawami' lights you will most certainly proceed to the great tawali' lights. It has been said that the lawa'ih lights are like meteors, the lawami' lights are like the Milky Way through clouds, and the tawali' lights are like the full view of the Northern Lights that fill the whole night sky.

The faqir's sole concern now, his all-consuming passion, is his Lord. Allah, glory be to Him, is not far, He is near. His nearness is nearer than the jugular vein – nearer, that is, than the thing is to itself. He is presence. Existence is presence, the Presence of Lordship. And that is light. Allah is the light of the heavens and the earth. That means of the inward and the outward. Of the sensory and the meaning. Of the sky and of the heart, which is the inner sky. Light upon light.

Allah guides whoever He wants to His light. Allah is in His slave's expectation of Him, so have a good expectation of Allah.

Praise belongs to Allah in every state.

Shawq – desire.

It is the heart's longing to meet with the Beloved. It is the delight of the heart as it moves towards its Lord. Desire ceases with arrival, but yearning and longing never end, for the heart of the lover will never be satisfied by one glance. More secrets will be sought for, more unveilings, more knowledges. And the gifts of the Beloved continue beyond our expectation or merit, and the secrets of the Beloved are endless.

Once the faqir experiences this longing and desire in the heart then immediately he realises that already what was dead has become alive. The heart is no longer the lump of flesh it was when he set out. Now it is the organ of transformation, the locus of lights, the screen of witnessing. He waits and he watches. He calls and he calls. He sings to his Beloved. He rises with the power of the dhikr. He sways. He moves forward in the circle. He enters the centre of the Dance. He dances for the Beloved. His whole being is consumed with passion. Every excuse is made to mention the Name. Every trace in existence points to evidence of the Beloved. The birds, the creatures, the oceans – all are coded meanings indicating the beauty of the Beloved or the majesty of the Beloved. It is no longer possible to look on an eagle or a mouse, a cat or a fish, let alone a man of Allah without the tears of love and recognition welling up from a living heart.

Dhawq – tasting.

The fruit of shawq is dhawq. Shaykh al-Akbar defines it as: 'The first of the beginnings of divine tajalliyat.'

The first dhawq will come in the company of the Shaykh by intense concentration on Allah in his presence. Dhawq will come upon the faqir in the sama'a, the singing of Diwan, and the Dance. When the heart tastes the first evidences from the source then it loses all awareness of the sensory existence. It dwells in meaning while the meaning lasts. There is no time, no Watcher to distract by false observation and 'outsideness'. The Watcher has been himself distracted. The Railer is powerless. The self is captive. The heart breaks free. Moves. Lives. Experiences. When the Wali of Bahlil met Shaykh al-'Alawi he said to him, 'Can you construct me a heart?' This is the passionate desire of the faqir who desires gnosis. By dhawq the heart comes into being as a live organ of spiritual awareness and knowledges.

Dhawq is life itself, for the first time breaking in. Or if you like – it is the first impulse of wakefulness after a long night of sleep. The sleeper awakes. Sleeps again. Stirs. This stirring precedes rising and full daylight experience after the night of ignorance.

Ash-Shurb – the drink.

Tasting by increase becomes drinking.

Shaykh al-Kamil in his great Diwan – 'My Beloved gave me a drink of the purity of love, and so I became beloved in every way.'

He also says:

'The Beloved gave us a draught of love to drink which forced all but the Beloved to vanish. We saw created beings as pure particles of dust: we saw the Lights openly emerge.'

It is in the nature of the drinking that there is increase in the meaning and therefore decrease in the sensory.

As you disappear lights appear. Of this condition Sidi Ali al-Jamal advised:

'Relax the intellect and learn to swim.'

Nothing will hold the lover back from tasting and drinking except impurities. When they are removed it is as if thought itself became a mark to be erased, however noble or however apposite. As the Sultan of the Lovers put it:

'In memory of the Beloved we quaffed a vintage that made us drunk before the creation of the vine!.'

Shaykh al-Akbar says of it: 'The middle of the tajalliyat whose ends are in every station.'

Sukr – drunkenness, intoxication. Drinking by increase becomes drunkenness.

Defined by Shaykh al-Akbar as: 'Withdrawal by a strong warid.'

Shaykh al-Harraq says in his noble Diwan:

'Resolution does not go to waste when you become intoxicated with the wine. It pours down the water of expansion on you in a tempest. You rock, shaking, dancing in joy, carried away. Your days are always green with wine.

When the sun shines in the intellect of its drinker, it makes created beings names for its essence.

When the glass leaves the wine, the flow of the lovers composes him. The colour of all shines.

The clever one recognised its limit by custom when he tasted from inside the jug. It is virgin.

They became drunkards. They did not break the seals because the state of the people of intelligence is beautiful when they are intoxicated.

No drinker among them ever broke the glass among the drinking companions, nor do they become light-headed.

If others divulge the secret, it protects them from the error of evil, outwardly and secretly.

They neither affirm nor reject what they have.

Perhaps they will seek shelter in the real business.

The essence negates them in reality while the light of the attribute affirms them. They are dead and alive.

They touched the drink with all the glasses. Clouds and clear skies will come to them.

They are the Men. May Allah make their glory endure forever! By Allah, others are nothing but rubbish and riffraff!'

Khamr – wine.

Shaykh al-Harraq says in his Diwan: 'You blame the wine foolishly. When someone's reality is cancelled out, then he becomes the wine.'

Sensory wine is the metaphor for its meaning-reality. The wine and the drunkenness are the same.

The famous definition by the Sultan of the Lovers in his Khamriyya is: 'They say to me, 'Describe it, for you know its description.' Yes, well do I know its attributes. Pure – but not water: subtle – but not air: luminous – but not fire: spirit – but not body.'

Shaykh Ibn al-Habib says in his Diwan:

'She did not leave until she had given him a drink from her goblet. There is no blame. Drink – for the wine is her speech.

And she is the Presence of the Truth, alone, who manifests herself with forms whose every light is different.'

Shaykh al-Fayturi says in the Fayturiyya:

'Draw near to the wine-jug of joy. Its drink is permitted! Truly you will be pleased with it – you will see the Face of Allah!'

Ka's – the cup.

One of the sufis has said: 'The cup is the heart of the Shaykh.'

Shaykh al-Fayturi says in the Fayturiyya:

'Al-'Alawi, the Ghawth of the age. My arrival was completed by him.

He is the glory of the secrets. He is the glass and the wine.

He is the cupbearer of the wine of perfection to the learned.

Al-Fayturi is out of his head with love from him – he drinks intoxicated from his wine.'

This language causes much confusion among the ignorant who make no attempt to understand meanings which are already so fine they have to be coded in the language of Ishara in the Diwans of the great gnostics. The whole language is clearly circling around the finer and finer distinction between the cup and the wine – the form and the light. We talk of 'the cups going round' – thus the sufis appear in the tavern, all faces become the face of the Shaykh. The face of the Shaykh in turn becomes a mirror with which to gaze into one's own secret. Drinking continues until the ecstasy overwhelms the drinker. Until the sun rises.

Sahwa – sobriety.

Shaykh al-Akbar defines it as: 'Returning to sensation after withdrawal by a strong warid.' It is a term introduced by our Imam Junayd. The scholars who talk and who do not taste have created arbitrary divisions in these matters so that there is a false idea that there is a school of sobriety over and against a school of drunkenness. The sufi is outwardly sober and inwardly drunk. He does not present himself as outwardly drunk while he is inwardly sober. Thus adab is always present by training and by intention. In the time of drinking and ecstasy Allah protects His loved ones by the noble company of His sadiqin. Thus the one who is unable to contain his ecstasy is not exposed to the view of the ignorant and those who censure, and the exception does not disprove the general rule. Imam Junayd rejected Hallaj from his circle, but his khalif was ash-Shibli, the great majdhoub – trained to hide his ecstasy in the deep suluk of his noble master. The Darqawi sets his heart on being one of outward sobriety but there is no question that the followers of Moulay al-Arabi ad-Darqawi are drunk/sober, as they are majestic/beautiful. They are beggar/kings as they are warrior/saints.

Farq: separation.

The time has come to take a vital pair of opposites and move them to a new and deeper set of terms. With this pair the earlier set of hiss and ma'na are invested with richer and more complex connotations. Its definition with the Shaykh al-Akbar is: 'It indicates creation without the Real. It is said that it is the contemplation of the worshipped.'

It is awareness of creation by creation. It is the single experiencing itself by multiplicity and thus reduced to multiplicity. Sidi Ali al-Jamal has said that sickness is farq, as health is gatheredness. In sickness one is aware of the body in its various functions, locations, nervous response and so on. The more sick one is the more awareness is trapped in separation, is earthed, grounded, spread out.

The sufis practice withdrawal from separation – not to be zahid and turn forever from the world – but in order to know it for what it is in the Real. Once the faqir has reached unitive knowledge then, as we say, separation will not veil him from gatheredness nor gatheredness from separation, and this does not mean a conceptual awareness but that the two cognitive and experiential realms will have unified as the sponge is unified field of sponge/water, without the sponge having become water or the water, sponge. Without, that is, any entering in or union or fusion or embodying. This withdrawal implies first turning from everything that appears as 'ghayr,' other, until at last you turn from yourself.

Jam': gatheredness. Shaykh al-Akbar says: 'It indicates Allah without creation.'

Withdrawal from separation will force the contemplator to withdraw, step by step from multiplicity. First by withdrawing from what does not hold and attract, and then from what does, which means the forms of the created existence, both gross and subtle, that is objects and thoughts, until the sea of their reflection is clear of the flotsam and jetsam of forms, and the currents of the self have subsided so that they look upon a clear reflective sea. Once the ocean is calmed there will arise from its depths, first its forms, and then its lights, and then its secrets. This second dimension of experience – which is first discovered in retreat and stillness – we call gatheredness. Later the condition of gatheredness will enter into the condition of discrimination. The goal is that the two should merge so that in all things outward and inward there is continual contemplation of the Beloved.

Sidi Ali al-Jamal says in *The Meaning of Man*: 'Election is in two divisions: election of separation and election of gatheredness. The election of separation is election from creation. The election of gatheredness is the election of the King, the Real. The one of separation obtains the kingdom of the Real, by the Real.'

Jam' al-Jam' – gatheredness of gatheredness. Defined by Shaykh al-Akbar as: 'Total consumption in Allah.'

Thus to the two terms farq and jam' there must now be added a third. The faqir is now in a position to grasp that if the deep unitary doctrine which he is approaching is to be total then there must be a way, still at this point inexplicable and ungraspable, in which we can confirm the reality without our being in it in any experiential way whatsoever. Allah confirming Allah on the tongue of Allah and not simply Allah confirmed on the tongue of His slave. Yet it must be understood that this is not an addition to the experience, a 'tying up' of unitary doctrine, or a forcing things to their 'logical conclusion.' Indeed the doctrine we approach has no business with logic or with illogic. Neither paradox nor contradiction can emerge with this teaching. It is known in the heart of the one who knows it, and is empty on the tongue of the one who speaks it. Jam' al-Jam' is the divine name of Al-'Alim on the tongue of the 'alim, it is the name of al-Wali on the tongue of the wali, and that from the place of knowledge and the circle of friendship, inaccessible, impenetrable, sealed off, the talisman of truth.

Tawhid – unity, its affirmation.

Our Imam said: 'It is a meaning which obliterates the outlines and joins the knowledges: Allah is as He always was. Tawhid has five pillars: it consists of the raising of the veil on the contingent, to attribute endlessness to Allah alone, to abandon friends, to leave one's country, and to forget what one knows and what one does not know.'

His greatest statement on tawhid, which Shaykh al-Akbar has called the highest of what may be said on the subject, is: 'The colour of the water is the colour of the glass.' Commenting on this Shaykh Ibn Ajiba said:

'This means that the exalted Essence is subtle, hidden and luminous. It appears in the outlines and the forms, it takes on their colours. Admit this and understand it if you do not taste it.'

Tawhid is itself a definition whose meaning is not complete for the one who holds to it until he has abandoned it or rather exhausted its indications and abandoned it for complete absorption in the One.

Tafrid – Isolation.

The meaning of tafrid is the doctrine of the experience as tawhid is the doctrine of knowledge of it. Tawhid belongs to the people of knowledge. Tafrid belongs to the people of dhawq. Yet again we note the passage from deep immersion in the teaching to deep immersion in the experience. Then, from that comes another doctrine which in turn encapsulates the lived or rather living experience of the people of gnosis.

Shaykh Ibn al-Habib says in his Diwan:

'The love of isolation will grant him continual realisation of aid which comes with the sakina (serenity).

He will begin to love Allah truly, without doubt, through seeing ihsan at every instant. Patience and a pure love without blemish contain all the Stations of Certainty.'

He also says:

'Power is only given to the one who has isolated himself with Him, and who, through much praise, is adorned with what pleases Him.

Thus he will continue to ascend in the deserts of His Essence until he is utterly annihilated in an annihilation that has nothing in it but loss.

If he returns to the existence-traces, he brings a robe of honour which proclaims his wilaya and glory.'

Af'al – the acts, being the actions of Allah. The af'al are the actions of Allah in the creation and the Command. This means both in the realm of particles, or whatever term may be used to indicate the basic materials of the Universe, as well as the organic identities. which are imbued with life. In the sufic cosmology, which is the sufi's own larger psychology, organism is not seen as separate from event. In other words each being is an event/organism as well as a place/organism for each living thing is an in-time creature as well as an in-space one. While it may be useful to describe 'wars' and 'societies' these do not have reality in the same way as the individuated organism.

Since all creation is under the divine Command, 'Kun!' all actions are the activity of One Actor. Qur'an says: 'Allah is the Creator of you and your actions.' While, from one viewpoint, you are answerable for your acts, from another, your actions follow from your in-time-placing and the givenness of your cellular reality. No one is free until they want what Allah wants. Then they will want, and what they want will always happen. Understanding this demands the removal of all projections onto the cosmic reality of concepts and value structures such as 'freedom of choice', 'unpredictability' and all the naive inventions of mathematical manipulation and its illusions of 'randomness.' Only one thing is happening, if you desire event, and it is the Universe.

Sidi Muhammad Ibn al-Habib says in his Diwan:

'You will journey from the cosmos to the Presence of Purity, and you will witness the Act of Allah in the creation and the Command.'

Sifat – attributes, being the attributes of Allah. When the seeker looks deeper to understand the myriad actions it can be perceived that all acts issue from attributes of capacity and potential. The core attributes are seven: speech, hearing, sight, knowledge, will, power, life. These are the core attributes of the human creature and in the transformative process of our perception by which we seek to penetrate to the secret of existence we return all our attributes, all creational and manifest attributes to their source in Oneness. Thus sight belongs to the Seer, speech to the Speaker, knowledge to the Knower, will to the Willer, power to the Powerful, and life to the Living.

The seeker must absorb into his awareness the recognition of the acts being as it were contained in the attributes, coming from them, emerging from them, for they were implied in them by their very coming out. When the Knower manifests He can only manifest knowing, so, the seeker moves from what is outwardly manifest of existence to what is hidden in it, from act to attribute. Tawhid confirms that Allah is One and therefore the seeker must grasp with a deep perceptive awareness that Allah is One in His acts and His attributes. What he now examines and prepares to understand he will soon see with clear seeing.

Shaykh Ibn al-Habib says in his Diwan:

'You will rise to the Names and drink of their light, so the attributes will appear to you without a veil.'

Dhat – the Essence, being the Essence of Allah. Allah is One. Before the creation of the Universe Allah was and there was nothing with Him. When he heard this, Imam Junayd exclaimed, 'Is – as He was!' Allah is One in His acts, His attributes and His essence, otherwise tawhid would not exist. Just as the attributes are the source of the acts, so the essence is the source of the attributes. Essence is present at every level. It is wrong to accuse the sufis of claiming they can 'know' essence alone. Allah cannot be divided for that too would destroy tawhid. What we recognise is that each aspect of being has a mode in which it is apprehended, and these modes are different. The gnostic seeks a stopping-place from 'difference' which will grant him direct perception of the Real. It is the secret of the Essence which is at the heart of the gnostic quest. It is that which unifies the opposites. The doctrine is not pantheist, for the universe has no permanent reality, although it is the seat of reality apprehended by the mode of the in-time. The doctrine is not monist for the slave is the slave and the Lord is the Lord, by the mode of the in-time. If there were no in-time there would be no Lordship. Unity is the declaration of Allah in His totality. But as Imam Junayd has noted: 'When the beyond time appears, the in-time is swallowed up in it.' Thus the meaning of the Essence manifests from the perfection of annihilation but remember the guidance of Shaykh al-Kamil when he said:

'Recognise the beauty of the Essence in every manifestation. Were it not for it – the existence of the Existent would not have been established.'

Ma'rifa – gnosis.

Gnosis is the knowledge on which all knowledge rests. All knowledges are suppositional yet verifiable in the realm of contingency. This knowledge is real yet not demonstrable. Other knowledges do not however illuminate their knower, nor remove his anguish, nor give him judgement in every case, nor invest his presence with light and radiance. The man of knowledges remains in needs and creational dependence. The man of gnosis does not remain in any need except dependency on his Lord who gives to him what he requires from creation. Other knowledges, being constructs without foundation, are baseless. Gnosis, the central knowledge, for it is knowledge of the self, is a proof to the one who knows it and this is its glory and its supremacy over all others. By it its possessor knows the Universe, how it is set up and its underlying laws in their action, their qualities and their essences. His knowledge of the Universe is his own self knowledge, while his knowledge of his own self is direct perception of his own original reality, his adamic identity. Everything he has comes from Allah. He never sees anything but he sees Allah in it, before it, after it. There is only Allah in his eyes as in his heart.

Whoever has gained this has gained the red sulphur.

By it he can transform the hearts of those who come to him, for his presence alone is a guidance and a reminder.

He guides to Allah by Allah.

Ism al-'Adham – the Supreme Name.

It is 'ALLAH' repeated in a designated fashion in accordance with the teaching of the Darqawi Way. It entails elongation of the Name, visualisation of the letters of the Name in the heart in the first maqam, stillness, and suspension of thought. All this is with idhn, permission, by one who is authorised.

The Name leads the seeker to the Named. The recitation of the Name is practiced alone, but its culmination is in isolation, either the isolation of the cave or of the khalwa. In the first maqamat the murid is guided by the Shaykh but when he reaches a certain point he must go on alone and from that moment the Shaykh follows after the murid, as it were, making plain what happens until the matter is complete, and it is direct witnessing of the Lord of creation. 'Ilm al-laduni – face to face knowledge.

It is the Name of Essence, and the greatest of the Names. If from A-L-L-A-H, that is alif lam lam ha – you remove the initial alif you are left with illah. If you remove the first lam you are left with lahu. If you remove the second lam it gives you Hu – which in its turn is the Name of Essence, Huwa. At every stage you find Allah.

Shaykh al-'Alawi counsels in his Diwan:

'Do dhikr of the Supreme Name, and cross through the cosmos, you will win the booty. Dive into the sea of out-of-timeness. This is the sea of Allah.'

Ghurba – exile.

Hadith declares: 'The search for the Real is an exile.' In the Diwan of Shaykh Ibn al-Habib, it says: 'By invocation of the god of the Throne you will become a zahid among men, and you will be annihilated from the nafs which delays you on the journey.' In this line he indicates the maqam of intense yearning which ultimately, when the time comes, which is Allah's time and no other – and it cannot be precipitated or withheld by any man – forces the seeker to turn from anything else which may have occupied him until then. He at this stage must put all from him that constitutes the world in the way of obligation, attraction, involvement and action. Having dispensed with his outward commitments, he is free to turn to the completion of his work. Unless he is utterly free in his break, and by his break, what follows may have no outcome, and Allah is the best of Judges and the only Knower of the secrets. In this matter the murid accepts the counsel of the Shaykh fulfilling his command if it is to khalwa and accepting its delay and guidance even if his passion for union seems over-powering. Trust in the Shaykh is never more vital to the seeker. In the end all doubts of oneself must be placed on the Shaykh as one big doubt. That must then express itself as conviction that one cannot arrive. This is the denial of the idhn of the Shaykh. Acceptance becomes the confirmation of the self in the Real by the Real. The Shaykh has from the beginning only been a mirror. This is never understood until arrival. Accept exile – it is the sunna of hijra.

Khalwa – retreat.

Khalwa, retreat, is the withdrawal from the world in the concentrated act of invocation of the Supreme Name in order to arrive at the vision of the Face. Its guide is the Shaykh. It is at this maqam that the words of Shaykh Mawlay Abdal-Oadir al-Jilani must be obeyed utterly. Ignorant people misquote them implying a false social control of the Shaykh over the murid. This is not so. It is within the context of this maqam that he says:

'Be with your Shaykh as a dead body in the hands of the washer.'

In khalwa all the adab of sitting well, of concentration, all the previous 'ubuda will serve the seeker. But nothing will serve so much as a great expectation of his Lord, a deep trust in the power and splendour of the One who can cover your bad qualities with His pure qualities, and your darkness with His light.

Shaykh Abu'l Abbas al-Mursi, the Qutb, said, 'It is difficult to reach the Shaykh. It is easy to reach Allah.' That is the secret of khalwa and the door to success. Cling to the Shaykh and tell him everything that happens with honesty and care. Follow his guidance to the last word in his command and his caution. Khalwa derives from a word meaning the wilderness, or the wide open space. Indeed for the gnostic it is the open space of open space.

'Uzla – retirement.

After khalwa – 'uzla. 'Uzla is the withdrawal after khalwa in order to fix in the heart the tremendous meanings and secrets that have burst upon the illuminated self. Often khalwa by the power of the tajalliyat that have descended and the force of the meanings that have burst upon the heart leaves the gnostic shattered, or still in intoxication – a fall-out from the impact of the annihilation.

'Uzla is a protection for the faqir for what must inevitably come next, but Allah knows best. In any event, it secures a clear understanding of what has happened, allows the gnostic to return to the world in humility and with his secret veiled from the common people.

Shaykh Ibn Ata-illah says in his Hikam:

'Bury your existence in the earth of obscurity, for whatever sprouts without having been buried first, flowers imperfectly.'

'Uzla should be practised often, by the one who is able, after khalwa. Its rules are less strict than the confinement of khalwa, some talk and isolated walking being permitted in it, as well as brief study.

Simsima – sesame. Shaykh al-Akbar defines simsima: 'Gnosis which is too fine to express.'

In gnosis – in its full sense of knowledge of Allah and His secrets – there are both stages of tremendous clarity, and stages of subtleties. Only the outlines of the journey have been hinted at by those who have gone before. Indeed, only some things may be said, some cannot be said. The silences of the gnostics are deeper in meanings than their speech. Of what has been written there are only indications. And of these much is in coded language as we have discovered in the great Diwans.

The gnostic will find and must be aware of gnoses that enter in and leave – once gone they are gone and cannot be held to any kind of inner formalising, yet they came and in the coming, as with all gnoses they alter the one who catches them on the wing. Thus, the gnostic realises that the secrets of love flow, and flow without end. It is in surrendering to this streaming of gnoses which may come upon the gnostic that one discovers great rewards lie in store. 'There are dates in the garden so gigantic that to encircle them is a year's journey, yet when the hand stretches out it takes it and eats it.'

Tajalli – manifestations. Allah's openings of vision on His slave. Illuminations.

The tajalliyat – sometimes called kashf – unveilings come upon the gnostic as he moves through the Malakut and the lights of the Jabarut break in upon him. As Shaykh al-Akbar noted, in reality Jabarut is not the highest kingdom but the middle kingdom, the barzakh or inter-space of lights, that is between the realm of forms that are hidden and the realm of forms that are visible to the outer eye. It is because in ordinary life, which is a sleep, we have no access to the hidden that the seeker has to work to turn from all that is (seen as) other-than-Allah. But this is in order to be able to view all of existence in the two worlds and see Allah by it. When the inner project dominates the outer then the invisible world takes over from the visible. The next stage of work is the aligning of the inner and the outer in significance. If one does not, one becomes a batinist thus denying the outer and limiting Allah. That is why the last phase preceding illumination is so difficult without guidance, if not impossible. 'There is no path to annihilation in Allah except on the hand of the Shaykh and the exception does not invalidate the rule,' said Shaykh al-Hashimi of Damascus. When the two are aligned, that is equal, then they cease to be opposites and thus they are annihilated for one no longer dominates the other. In this phase the lights of the attributes emerge openly. As the recognition dawns the light – the great light of the Essence emerges. The tajalli of the Essence. The Face of the Beloved.

Takhalli – relinquishment. This is the last defeat of dunya, of the world as illusion. Once the gnostic has tasted the tajalliyat and drunk of their lights then what had once mattered becomes small in his eyes. After a brief or long period of disintoxication brought about through the secret of the Decree, the gnostic begins to yearn for greater unveilings and greater initiation into secrets now that he has contacted his own innermost self, now that he has entered the audience chamber and may speak with the Beloved. As a result of this what comes to him of the outward world diminishes in significance as the treasure-chests of his own inwardness reveal their treasure.

Due to this new distaste for the learning which is devoid of gnoses the man of knowledge takes on relinquishment. Its fruits are wisdom, ease of existence, provision by miracle, followers without seeking them, and love from the creation, both human and animal. Far from cutting off from the world, he finds that as he once sought the world and it eluded him, as Mawlay al-'Arabi, our Master, noted, now the world seeks him and finds him. But in everything he sees his Master. He gives everything its due. His heart is free.

Al-'Ama – the great mist.

In Tirmidhi is the noble hadith where the Messenger is asked: 'Where was Allah before the creation of the Universe?' He replied: 'He was in the 'Ama.' It goes on to say that it had no aboveness or belowness. In other words it was a primordial non-spatiality in non-time. Sayyidina Ali, Allah ennoble his face, was asked the same question and after a long silence he said: 'To ask where was Allah is to ask of a place. Now Allah was – but there was no space. Then he created time/space and He is now as He was before time/space.'

Thus the 'Ama is an emptiness without forms in it, utterly void, non-existence. The original void. At a stage in the deep contemplation of the gnostics on their way to Allah, they enter, if Allah wills it, into the great dark mist of non-differentiation. Beforetimeness. Shaykh Ibn al-Habib counsels:

Oh you who desire the presence of being an eyewitness, you must rise above the spirit and the forms.

'And cling to the original void – and be as if you were not – oh annihilated one!

Truly you will see a secret whose meanings have spread in every age.'

Muraqaba – watching.

The watching began when the faqir guarded against the wrong actions of the self. Then the watching deepened to an attention in fikr which prevented anything 'other' entering into the awareness. However there is a final stage of watching which is the summit of gnosis. It envelops the dislocation of awareness which is the experience of unity. Let us look again. In stage one you set up a Watcher to watch the outward and make it pure. In the second stage the Watcher watches the self in its inward deceptions. From this emerges a profound stage in which the Watcher is voided of any thing or form to watch, held only by the act of calling on the Name. This leads to the Original Void. Then the seeker moves between the worlds, drawing sensory and meaning into closer and closer, finer and finer balance. When light dawns you *know* that you do not see Allah, but Allah sees you. Ihsan. This is not 'pure monism' or any other simplistic philosophical position – it is a situation that cannot be expressed in linear expression or formulae for it is subtle, dynamic and secret. The wird of this time is the Wird-as-Sahl.

Allahu ma'ee. Allahu nadhirun ilayya.

Allahu shahidun 'alayya. 66 times.

Mushahada. Witnessing.

Shaykh al-Fayturi said: 'The secret of watching is witnessing.'

Shaykh Ibn al-Habib said in his Diwan:

'The Merciful is only to be seen in manifestations such as the Throne, the Footstool, the Tablet of forms, or the Lote-tree.'

He also says:

'The Real is only seen in manifestation whether by an angel or by mortal man. The first manifestation is the Light of Ahmad, may the most excellent of blessings be upon him eternally.'

He continues, and take this in most carefully –

'By him the Real has filled every creature and all that is or was,

So see him in the self and on the horizon, and join that to perception of the Creator, And that seeing will make up for every defect in the self, the heart and the hidden of the hidden.'

Thus the gnostic moves from the tajalliyat of the Attributes to the tajalli of the Essence.

The end is direct vision of the Face.

Shaykh Ibn al-Habib said:

'The face of the Beloved appeared and shone in the early dawn.'

Wilayat – Friendship with Allah, acceptance. Wilayat is the station of the wali – he is the one who sits in knowledge. Shaykh Ibn al-Habib says in his Diwan:

'You will become one who sits with Allah, without ceremony, and you will be safe from doubt, shirk, and otherness.'

Shaykh Ibn Ajiba says of this:

'Its fruit is the realisation of annihilation in the Essence after the disappearance of the sensory. What was wiped out never had any existence, and what remains never has any end.'

Ibrahim bin Adham said once to a man: 'Do you wish to be a wali?' The man replied, 'Yes.' 'Then do not desire anything of this world or the next. Dedicate yourself to Allah, turn your face to Him: He will treat you with gentleness and aid you.'

Fana' – annihilation in Allah.

Shaykh al-Akbar says: 'The slave sees by his action that Allah preserves that.'

The three stages of annihilation are outlined in the Diwan of Shaykh Ibn al-Habib:

'So the oneness of action appears at the beginning of dhikr of Allah.

And the oneness of attribute comes from love of Allah.

And the oneness of His Essence gives going-on in Allah.'

That is: annihilation in the Act: annihilation in the Attributes: annihilation in the Essence.

Shaykh al-'Alawi guides in his Diwan:

'The Mulk and the Malakut as well as the Jabarut are all attributes, and the Essence designates Him. Withdraw from the Attributes and annihilate yourself in the essence of the essence. These are indications whose end leads to Allah.'

Fana' means exactly what it says. It is the meaning-death, based on the cessation of the attributes, even life itself. It is arrived at by the most fine process of withdrawal from the sensory by the means of the Supreme Name until even the Name, the last contact with awareness disappears. From the depth of the Original Void the secrets and the lights emerge. The seeker will pass through the heavens, each with its own colour and meanings. Light upon light. Until the great tajalli which unveils the secret and indicates Allah.

'The meaning of the Essence will be manifested from the perfection of annihilation, so you will have going-on, rich with Allah for the rest your life!'

Bala – trial. After fana' comes bala. After annihilation comes trial. The impact of the gnostic illumination is so devastating, and so burns up the locus of the self, that it is possible that its impact can throw the one who has returned from it off balance. He may imagine that somehow the whole experience is his doing, that there has been some achievement and the very meaning of the unveiling will be reversed by the deception of suddenly re-entering the sensory. It is by clinging to helplessness and never losing sight of the essential doctrine – the slave is the slave and the Lord is the Lord – that the traveller will gain the victory. The matter does not end with fana' although it is its climax and key.

Imam Junayd has warned that the gift that follows it is bala to purify the slave in his new situation and to adjust the lens of his new vision. To the one who has joined the opposites in the vision, a re-education is necessary to begin to make these meanings live while functioning in the sensory. Allah's is the gift of trials on His slave, for his protection, and recovery. Allah is the Merciful and Compassionate. He is the Near. Now immediately comes the first test of the lover not to reject Him when He appears in terrible Majesty.

Baqa' – going-on. Going-on in Allah.

Shaykh al-Akbar says: 'The slave sees that Allah preserves everything.' After bala – baqa'. The word derives from one of the names of Allah, al-Baqi'u, for He is the Ever-continuing. Thus the slave returns to slavehood. In the sublime statement of Shaykh Ibn Ata'lllah:

'Allahumma, You have commanded me to return to created things, so return me to them robed in lights and the guidance of inner sight, so that I may return from them to You just as I entered in to You from them, with my secret protected from looking at them and my himma raised above dependence on them. For truly, You have power over everything.'

This is the magisterial declaration of baqa'.

Baqa' is the return to the slavery of beginnings, with the outward a confirmation of the beginning, the Path and the arrival, with the secret hidden and the knowledge wrapped in a talisman. The man of baqa' is outwardly slave, inwardly free, outwardly dark, inwardly illuminated, outwardly sober, inwardly drunk. He is the barzakh of the two oceans – the shari'at and the haqiqat. Separation does not veil him from gatheredness and gatheredness does not veil him from separation.

Sahq – pulverisation.

Shaykh al-Akbar calls this: 'The disappearance of your structure under force.' Mahq he calls: 'Your annihilation in His source. It means destruction. Sa'iqa – thunderbolt. Annihilation in the divine tajalli.'

These three terms differently confront the central event of fana' which must not be underestimated, for the power of Allah is mighty, and the annihilation of the core experience, or simply of the locus, is a shattering thing for which these terms are exact and not exaggerated. Within the deep contemplation of the gnostic when the time comes and he is ordered to move with an inner impulse of the heart – then at that time which is non-time – the impact of this breaking of the time barrier is the thunderbolt which cannot be avoided. While it is described in these terms, pulverisation and destruction, it must be remembered that He who is Aziz is also Ar-Rahman. At this stage the lover's yearning is nothing less than to die, to be done with the shadow self and at last be face to face with the Real – 'Ilm al-laduni – direct knowledge. This is its price, but oh gnostic! remember when you return to the world, that was your reality, so what are you to do now unless it is constantly to praise Him.

'Everyone that is on it will be annihilated. And there goes-on only the Face of your Lord of Majesty and Generous   Gifts.'

Nasut – manhood.

We have arrived at the triad which designates existence from the new position of knowledge that belongs to the gnostic. Before gnosis the Universe was outside him – opposite him. In the secrecy of his muraqaba he rolled up the Universe within him and went beyond. He has confirmed the great statement of Shaykh Sidi 'Ali al-Jamal: 'Existence is your separation and you are its gatheredness.' It is no longer possible from his own point of view to speak of the cosmos in its out-thereness. Nasut is a term which defines man as a cosmic gatheredness. Now man is man/cosmos. The gnostic is a universal man. So his manhood is in this englobing aspect of his awareness. He no longer has a psychology yet he continues to exist. Equally the world no longer has a cosmology for he knows the universal reality in his inwardness. For him, travel outwardly in space is a kind of ignorance if embarked on as such, for outward travel is to discover the self, just as he found that inward travel was to discover the cosmic event.

So we may say that nasut is the first of a new triad of knowing, a mode of knowing existence in which the cogniser and his field are not two, or conjoined, but one bilateral reality.

Lahut – godhood.

This is the second term in the new series. By it the realm of Allah's power and dominion, his lordship – rububiyyat – over existence in its inward aspect is defined. Lahut, being the realm of Allah's meanings and source-forms 'ayn ath-thabitah is also the realm of the gnostic's own source and the source of his source. Thus gatheredness – his gatheredness by knowledge – is that reality in which dwells his source as well as the source of all the known things and the unknown things. Only nothing is hidden from him – but still he is only permitted knowledges according to his capacity and the gift the capacity is. This is the evidence of his slavehood and His lordship. Yet the gnostic in his helplessness swims in the ocean of knowledge and grasps the sword of wisdom. He is mighty in his weakness and wise in his ignorance. He is radiant and given a tongue from his own humanity and his silence. Lahut is his gatheredness, and it is the one ocean of the secrets without any separation or division.

Rahamut – sourcehood.

The Presence of Mercy. This is the third term. As the second indicates the gnostic in his aspect towards his lahut which is hidden, that is the realm of all the source-forms and thus his own – so there must be a term in which these two aspects unify. Thus the source-hood of the self/cosmos is the unifying secret which joins the majesty and the beauty in Unity. This is the reality of compassion and subtlety, all-pervasiveness. In other words we have replaced a concept of essence with a gnosis of the Real.

It is only from the rahamut that the gnostic who returns may declare with direct proof from his journey that the compassionate Lord is not separated from His qadar – His decree – and its secret – 'I send people to the Garden and I do not care. I send people to the Fire and I do not care.'

In nasut, lahut and rahamut, gnoses are gathered, insights are confirmed, and realms of worlds disappear into one another, are swallowed up, no longer remain. Allah was and there was nothing with Him. Is – as He was.

Mahabba – love.

The gnostic is entering into love in its fullness. Its beginning was suluk, its middle was jadhb and fana'. Its end is baqa'.

The secrets of love flow endlessly. The gnostic finds gift upon gift from the Beloved. Just as in the beginning of his affair Allah covered his wrong actions and hid them from His compassion now the Lord uncovers to the people his lights and knowledges so that people turn to him as he once turned from people. As love once flowed in his heart for the fuqara' and the people of trial now Allah causes love to flow in their hearts for him. As He overwhelmed him then with baraka so He does now, with more.

What once he judged harshly in others now he forgives, and his heart flows with mercy. Where before he could not guide people to right action even by good counsel now he purifies hearts of what makes them sick by his glance. Once unification was in his inward now it becomes manifest in his outward.

Of this Shakyh Ibn Ata'illah says: 'The lights of the wise precede their words, so that, wherever being illuminated occurs, the expression arrives there.'

Qurb – nearness.

In his sublime and incomparable song in 'The Desire of the Wayfaring Murids and the Jewel of the Gnostic Travellers', its author says: defining the Station of Nearness –

'Invocation of the Beloved clothed us in beauty, radiance, exaltation and joy. In drawing near we threw off all restraint and proclaimed the One we love to glorify. The Beloved gave us a draught of love to drink which forced all but the Beloved to vanish. We saw created beings as pure particles of dust: we saw the lights openly appear. After having been obliterated and annihilated in a light-giving wine, we returned to creation. By a bounty from Allah we were given going-on and with patience we concealed the One we love. How often have we looked upon a wayfarer so that he has risen to the stations of those who have plunged into the seas.'

In this Shaykh Ibn al-Habib reveals the gifts reserved for those who enter into the intimacy of the station of nearness. It is the station of 'within two bows-lengths' – a term that is understood by the gnostics in its indication of closeness and face-to-face meeting, the secret centre of Unity itself. The one of this station now is active in the inner as before he was active in the outer. Before he travelled looking for lovers of Allah, now he travels inwardly looking to return to the Beloved. The song continues:

'We concerned ourselves with something secretly, and so it was, and the One we chose to love has come to us.'

Taraqqi is rising. Talaqqi is receiving.

The first is defined by Shaykh al-Akbar as: 'Moving in states, stations, and gnoses.' The second as: 'Your taking what comes to you from Allah.'

The gnostic does not cease in his journey, only now the journey is in Allah by Allah with awareness and tasting and drinking and ecstasy and discovery and unveiling upon unveiling according to the asking and the gifts of the Beloved.

It is in these states that the gnostic finds at last a delight that was not among those things he yearned or even hoped for – for this delight is a gift from Allah the existence of which he did not know, and indeed could not have known. For there is no means to its indication and no means to its delineation. It is known by those who know it and it is the delight of those who delight in it. It is constant discovery. It is constant renewal. It is ever fresh witnessing of the beauty and ever fresh bowing to the majesty. So a time comes upon the gnostic when he realises that man himself was not what he had thought, in his wickedness and narrowness and cruelties. Man is vast, is capable of a state unbounded. This brings to birth in the gnostic a new longing and joy – to transmit to the sons of Adam the good news and the warning – and to invite people to the way of self-knowledge, witnessing and wonders.

Lisan – tongue.

Shaykh al-Akbar says it is: 'That by which divine eloquence occurs to the ears of the gnostics.'

For the people of love the gifts of Allah flow endlessly. The strong gnostic who is constant in his return to the audience chamber of witnessing will find that Allah honours His slaves by His speech as well as by His unveilings. So Allah speaks directly and in accordance with the indications expressed in the Qur'an. Just as vision has its adab, that is unequivocal, between the Lord and the slave, so too does audition.

This is sometimes called the removal of the sandals – for the slave puts away the two worlds before he speaks with the Beloved and hears the Beloved. It is a place – and that place is a presence – hadrat ar-Rabbani – the presence of Lordship. These presences increase and their meanings increase until the great gnostic soon is decoding message after message from his Beloved. Thus what at first is within the intimacy of the khalwa, and the 'uzla may soon take place in the courtyard and in the market place. Allah is the Hearer. Allah is the Speaker. Allah is the Lord of the Universe.

Glory be to Him.

Tamkin – fixity.

Shaykh al-Akbar defines it: 'With us, it is being firm in talwin. It is said to be the state of the people of arrival.' Once the gnostic is established in his station, and within it has deepened and enriched his gnosis by much return and much drinking at the source and increase of thanks, and praise, and watching and witnessing, and taking from the many gifts of the Giver – then this vast and tremendous being, whose human attributes slowly disappear and fall away with the radiance of his going-on, rich in Allah, becomes fixed in his new dynamic state of receiving the gifts of the Lord. It is remaining in receptivity, fixed in acceptance of the overwhelming generosity of a Lord whose bounty and magnanimity knows no end. It is the clarity of those who persist in recognising Allah in whatever comes of trial and delight and acknowledge only one truth in all of it. To the one of tamkin this life lasts only one hour – and the vast in-time is swallowed up at every instant by the beyond-time.

Taste the fixity of the man of fixity and it will move you on your journey to Allah.

May Allah take you to its noble station and its glorious gifts. Allahu akbar.

Talwin – change.

Shaykh al-Akbar defines it: 'The slave's moving in his states. With most, it is the station of decrease. With us it is the most perfect of stations. The slave's state in it is the state of the word of Allah-ta'ala: 'Every day He is engaged in some affair.' Shaykh ash-Shushtari said: 'My goal in love is to be in change.' Change is the secret of Allah in existence, the station of the great Barzakh. It is complete submission. It is the maqam as-salat outwardly and the maqam al-uns inwardly. Outwardly prayer, inwardly intimacy. It is not to look out on the creation but that you see the secrets of Allah. It is not to look in on the self but that you see the secrets of creation. It is the condition of pure helplessness in the station of power. It is the station of A'isha who declared, 'Would that I were a leaf upon that tree.' Its full reality is to be in talwin with tamkin and its opposite. These two are one station. It is what Rumi called the spinning top which seems still to the beholder because it moves so fast. Once you have achieved this you have reached the limits of what the human being may reach – you are among the elect of the elect of the elite. The people of this splendour are a community, some known, some hidden.

Afrad – individuals.

They are defined by the greatest teacher thus: 'It designates the men outside the jurisdiction of the Qutb!'

We now reach the last that need be known or can be known of the human situation in knowledge from the viewpoint of the Real and the instructions of the Real to the great, all this in accordance with the secrets unveiled in the Qur'an on the tongue of the Messenger, blessing of Allah and peace be upon him.

Know that as the ants are nations like yourselves, so in the inward, man is arranged with structure and patterning according to the same divine beauty and order of shape and flux. Yet since everything in creation is in turbulent movement so this ordering is not strict any more than the numbering of petals is. There is a norm and there are differences. The afrad are those who function outside this divine unfolding of great and complete men in gnosis and power. The afrad are those glorious ones who do not fall within the obligations of obedience, or helpless and unquestioning recognition of the Man of the time. No one denies or may deny the afrad although the afrad may deny the Qutb. Shaykh ai-Fayturi declares in the Fayturiyya:

'I am an individual of the age, a slave without interruption.'

300 Nuqaba – The chiefs.

Shaykh al-Akbar says: 'They are those who extract the hidden things of the selves. They are three hundred'.

They are the people who transform ignorant human beings into human beings – who take people from darkness to the gift of Allah, which is light from Him and by Him not by them or from them. They are the people of the red sulphur – the alchemist's gold. Some transform hearts by their art and others transform base metal into gold, and others do both. Between them there is recognition and reticence. There is adab and amazement at the differences Allah has created among his knowing slaves, and delight in this. Nothing and no-one will remove them from the station of adab. Their adab among each other is famous. Their communication, of a subtlety so fine it is often un-noticed. Some are hidden in the deserts in poverty and in need. Others are placed before men for all the world to see. Yet not one of them but that he basks in the vision of Allah as the great sea lions who are their sign between the land and the ocean bask on the shore. Each shares the same dhikr.

Hu! Hu! Hu!

40 Nujaba – the nobles.

From the nuqaba are forty nobles. Of them Shaykh al-Akbar notes: 'They are forty. They are occupied with hearing the burdens of creation, and they only move for the right of another.'

See in this the compassion of the Lord for his creation. Our Messenger Muhammad, the first of the gnostics, blessings and peace be upon him, said: 'There will always be forty of my people of the nature of Ibrahim.' Thus the inner core of the nuqaba are marked by their concern and their lowly service to others. They are the servants of the poor. They are near in copying the sunna of the Messenger in deep love of the masakin, the bereft, and the troubled. Their sign by which they are recognised is their utter reliance on supplications over every other kind of 'ibada and it is their sunna, their dhikr, and their reflection. By it they live and by it they help. Some dwell in an ayat and some dwell in a surat and some swim in the Qur'an. Some live uniquely on the secrets of Fatihah.

7 Abdal. The substitutes.

Shaykh al-Akbar says: 'They are seven. Whoever travels from a place while he leaves his body in its form so that no one recognises that he has gone, that one is a badl and none other. He is modelled on the heart of Ibrahim, peace be upon him.' Declaring their high station Shaykh Ibn al-Habib says:

'The Path of the Abdal dedicated to Allah is – hunger, sleeplessness, silence, isolation, and dhikr.' This is a statement confirmed by all the great awliya.

Just as the common people talk endlessly about miracles while they are commonplace among the salihun – so knowledge and identification of the abdal and those beyond them are talked of and denied by the sadiqun. But there is no doubt. They are there. Here and there. They are to the cosmos as the heart is to the body. If it were to perish the body would perish for it is its life and meaning. It is not that there is no news of them. There is. But it is from the truthful, of the truthful, on the tongue of the Truth, not from the ignorant on the tongue of gossip. The abdal – even they do not indicate the limit of spiritual capacity.

4 Awtad. The four pillars.

They are the four pillars, or pegs, taken from the seven abdal.

The Shaykh al-Akbar says of them:

'It designates the four men whose stages are according to the stages of the four pillars. If there is east, west, north, and south from the world, each of them has a station for that direction.'

This is the nucleic centre of sufic wisdom. They are four and when one dies another moves to take his place. They are known. I confirm that they are not only the supports of the four corners of the globe but that in the Unseen they are the supports of the Ka'ba, the House of Allah itself. For the House is the House of Allah in the outward but in the inward the house of Allah is the heart of, or the hearts of, the believers. Allahu 'alim.

2 Imams.

Shaykh al-Akbar says: 'They are two individuals. One of them is on the right of the Ghawth, and his jurisdiction is in the Malakut. The other is on his left and his jurisdiction is in the Mulk. He is higher than his companion. He is the one who succeeds the Ghawth.'

See the perfection of the patterning on the hidden side of things as you see the perfection of the visible side of things. 'You will not find any flaw in Allah's creation.' Here, of the two rulers of spiritual realities, each dominates from one aspect. So one has one task and another another.

Recognition is confirmation, and non-recognition is not a proof against them.

If you have not perceived the patterning with which His beauty shapes the outward you will never be able to recognise it in the inward. There is no difference. Each world is opposite the other. The human realm lies between the two worlds, thus one aspect of it is visible and may be analysed, but another is hidden and may only be recognised by the sciences of the ones who know this Path. And Allah is the only Knower.

Qutb – the axis. The Pole.

And from these two is one. He is the Qutb. Shaykh al-Akbar says: 'He is the Ghawth. It designates the one who is the place whereby Allah surveys the world in every age. He is modelled on the heart of Israfil, peace be upon him.'

The Sultan of the Lovers declared:

'Therefore it is on me the heavens turn, and wonder then at their Qutb which encompasses them even though he is a central point.' The world swirls around him, the Universe of stars take their meaning and place from his sublime centrality of stillness and adoration. With him only Allah's sublimity is apparent. His tongue speaks only of Allah's wisdom and Allah's power. He glorifies Allah in every situation.

He declared: 'The relationship of the Seal and the Poles to his Light is that of a drop to oceans of light and refreshment.' Here Shaykh Ibn al-Habib, Pole of his time, indicated the relationship between these sublime gnostics and the Messenger Muhammad's light. He also confirmed the declaration of the Mashishiyya:

'Oh Allah, he is Your all-embracing Secret, guiding to You, by You, and Your mightiest veil standing before You.'

Sukun – Stillness.

The mark in grammar indicating no vowel following a consonant, thus silence. This is the heart of the Qutb. There are, of course, the aqtab and the Qutb. That is, there are those who have reached the station of sukun and there is that one who is over all the others of his time as Shaykh Ibn al-Habib put it, 'whether they know it or not.' If a man says he is a qutb he is a qutb. But the one who is the Outb of the aqtab will have a court as a king does, and a jurisdiction as a king does of spiritual realities however, not of earthly ones. He is the one who is generous with his secret. This sukun, this stillness is not a state, but his condition, filling him both in jihad and in contemplation. His heart may beat fast, he may taste the excitement of the battle, but his stillness rules him and he drinks of the vision of the Face and he glorifies Allah. Oh what praise and what glorification may pour from the heart of a man. To deny the Qutb is only to deny your own capacity for centrality to the secrets of existence. It is the badge of ignorance, as his acknowledgement of each and every one is the badge of his lights and gnoses. Allah give us love for the awliya of Allah and their elite. Amin.

The Sultan of the Lovers said:

'Therefore struggle with yourself that you may see in you, and from you, a peace beyond what I have described a serenity born of emptiness.'

Tajrid – Stripping away.

The complete and perfect man is not recognised unless you see him in his confirmation of the beginnings. He is the voice of beginnings as he is the secret of ends. His simplicity of teaching is the depths of his knowledge. His reality is such by his calling to tajrid for it is the Path and it has always been the Path and there is no new jurisdiction in the hidden as there is no new juridiction in the seen. Sidi Ali al-Jamal says in this matter:

'The one who is zahid in this world is the one who recognises Allah in its retreat and its advance.'

So we say that the people of this noble Path will always be marked by the noble character of the one who is their guide and their Light, the Messenger Muhammad, may the blessings of Allah and His peace be upon him according to the number of created things. For this reason the one on it is called faqir from beginning to end. If you seek power or renown or reward from men by this Path then know that it has in it nothing but sorrow for you. If you set out seeking the Face of Allah then know that Allah is the Answerer of our prayers and His mercy is beyond our mercy, or our understanding of mercy. The Path is pure compassion at its beginning and at its end. One who knows that will be content with tajrid and rich in it, a king even if Allah puts him in rags, as he will remain a faqir even if Allah robes him in the robes of a king. Every king dies like a faqir while every faqir dies like a king.

Kamal – perfect.

The Perfect Man is not perfect in any way other than that his gnosis is perfect and by it his life is preserved by Allah. On being asked if such a man was free from committing wrong actions Imam Junayd gave the profound answer: 'The command of Allah is a decree determined.'   (33:38)

The Sultan of the Lovers said of the perfect one:

'For my meeting is my parting, and my nearness is my being far, and my fondness is my aversion, and my end is my beginnings.'

Shaykh Ibn 'Ata-illah said of him:

'He drinks and increases in sobriety. He is absent and increases in presence. His gatheredness does not veil him from his separation, nor does his separation veil him from his gatheredness. His annihilation does not divert him from his going-on, nor does his going-on divert him from his annihilation. He acts justly towards everyone and gives everyone his proper due.'

This is the possibility of the human creature. This is the capacity of the one possessed of a core. Recognise your perfection from the place of recognition. Praise belongs to Allah at the beginning and at the end. There is no power and no strength but from Allah, the Exalted, the Vast.

THE TREASURY OF TRUTHS

Oh Allah, bless and grant peace to our Lord and Master Muhammad, the first of the Lights emanating from the oceans of the sublimity of the Essence. With every one of Your perfections in all Your tajalliyat in the two worlds – the hidden and the seen – he realises the meanings of the Names and Attributes. He is the first to give praise and worship with every kind of adoration and good action. He is the helper of all created beings in the world of forms and the world of spirits. And blessings be upon his family and companions with a blessing that will lift the veil from his noble face for us in visions and in the waking state, and will acquaint us with You and with him in all ranks and presences. Be gracious to us, oh Mawlana, by his rank, in movement and in stillness, in looks and in thoughts.'

****

Glory be to your Lord, the Lord of Might, above all that they describe, and peace be upon the Messengers, and praise belongs to Allah, the Lord of the worlds.

The Isnad of the Tariq

Sayyiduna
Muhammad
blessings and peace of Allah be upon him

Sayyiduna 'Ali ibn Abi Talib

In the name of Allah,
All-Merciful,
Most Merciful
Say: 'He is Allah,
Absolute Oneness,
Allah, the Everlasting
Sustainer of all.
He has not given birth
and was not born.
And no one is
comparable to Him.'

Sayyidi al-Hasan ibn 'Ali
Sayyidi Abu Muhammad Jabir
Sayyidi Sa'id al-Ghazwani
Sayyidi Fathu's-Su'ud
Sayyidi Sa'd
Sayyidi Sa'id
Sayyidi Ahmad al-Marwani
Sayyidi Ibrahim al-Basri
Sayyidi Zaynu'd-Din al-Qazwini
Sayyidi Muhammad Shamsu'd-Din
Sayyidi Muhammad Taju'd-Din
Sayyidi Nuru'd-Din Abu'l-Hasan 'Ali
Sayyidi Fakhru'd-Din
Sayyidi Taqiyyu'd-Din

Sayyidi al-Hasan al-Basri
Sayyidi Habib al-'Ajami
Sayyidi Da'ud at-Ta'i
Sayyidi Ma'ruf al-Karkhi
Sayyidi Sari as-Saqati
al-Imam al-Junayd
Sayyidi ash-Shibli
Sayyidi at-Tartusi
Sayyidi Abu-l-Hasan al-Hukkari
Sayyidi Abu Sa'id al-Mubarak
Mawlana 'Abd al-Qadir al-Jilani
Sayyidi Abu Madyan al-Ghawth
Sayyidi Muhammad Salih
Sayyidi Muhammad ibn Harazim
Sayyidi 'Abd ar-Rahman al-'Attar
Sayyidi 'Abdu's-Salam ibn Mashish
Sayyidi Abu'l-Hasan ash-Shadhili
Sayyidi Abu'l-'Abbas al-Mursi
Sayyidi Ahmad ibn 'Ata'illah
Sayyidi Da'ud al-Bakhili
Sayyidi Muhammad Wafa
Sayyidi 'Ali Wafa
Sayyidi Yahya al-Qadiri
Sayyidi Ahmad al-Hadrami
Sayyidi Ahmad Zarruq
Sayyidi Ibrahim al-Fahham
Sayyidi 'Ali ad-Dawwar
Sayyidi 'Abd ar-Rahman al-Majdhub
Sayyidi Yusuf al-Fasi
Sayyidi Muhammad ibn 'Abdillah
Sayyidi Qasim al-Khassasi
Sayyidi Ahmad ibn 'Abdillah
Sayyidi al-'Arabi ibn 'Abdillah
Sayyidi 'Ali al-Jamal
Mawlana al-'Arabi ibn Ahmad ad-Darqawi

Sayyidi Abu Ya'za al-Muhaji
Sayyidi Muhammad 'Abd al-Qadir al-Basha
Sayyidi Muhammad ibn Qudur
Sayyidi ibn al-Habib al-Buzidi
Mawlana Ahmad ibn Mustafa al-'Alawi
Sayyidi Muhammad al-Fayturi Hamuda

A man came running
from the far side of
the city, saying, 'My
people! follow the
Messengers!'

Sayyidi Ahmad al-Badawi
Sayyidi Muhammad al-'Arabi
Sayyidi al-'Arabi al-Hawwari
Sayyidi Muhammad ibn 'Ali
Sayyidi Muhammad ibn al-Habib

Sayyidi 'Abdalqadir as-Sufi